Good Grammar!

Peter Clutterbuck

⒰PPER PRIMARY

Meaningful activities that
make grammar easy
for Upper Primary

Blake
EDUCATION
Better ways to learn

GW01425292

© 1998 Peter Clutterbuck
Reprinted 1999, 2001, 2003, 2006

ISBN 1 86509 104 9
Good Grammar! Book 3

Blake Education
Locked Bag 2022
Glebe NSW 2037

Editor: Sharon Dalgleish.
Cover by Love of Design.
Designed and typeset by The Modern Art Production Group.
Printed in Singapore by Green Giant Press

ii

The material in this book can be reproduced by the original purchaser for use with their class(es) only.

Introduction

This third book of **Good Grammar!** provides Upper Primary teachers with resources, activities and ideas aimed at consolidating and extending children's knowledge of grammar. The activity pages can be used as a resource around which to build and develop a classroom program.

Good grammar skills help children improve their expression and give them an appreciation of how the various elements of English are used to convey meaning. With an understanding of the rules, processes and elements that govern English, children are able to communicate both correctly and effectively.

In the past, lessons in grammar often became irrelevant and meaningless to children because of the tendency to stress the elements rather than focus on the function of the elements. **Good Grammar!** ensures that the functions of elements such as parts of speech, phrases and sentences are related to expression in a practical and purposeful way.

Good Grammar! is designed to make it as easy as possible to find what you need. Photocopiable worksheets are grouped according to grammatical element, and each of these elements is introduced with a definition and examples for the teacher, followed by a collection of appropriate and fun teaching strategies. With the three books in **Good Grammar!** teachers can create an individual and comprehensive grammar program.

Contents

How to Use This Book

The Good Grammar! series aims to improve children's ability to:
- **use language effectively in their own writing,**
- **use language accurately in their own writing,**
- **read critically the writing of others.**

With this in mind, the books have been designed to make it easy for teachers to find:

The grammatical elements to teach at each level
- refer to the overview provided by the assessment checklist,
- read the background information to find the terminology and depth of treatment appropriate.

Concise background information about each grammatical element
- located in the introduction to each grammatical element.

Practical strategies showing how to teach each grammatical element
- use fun activities as starting points to introduce a grammatical element and capture children's interest,
- use other proven strategies to explicitly teach or model a grammatical element,
- use games for reinforcement.

Blackline master worksheets to reinforce learning
- a comprehensive resource around which to build a program.

Systematic teaching

Children need a solid general framework of grammatical understanding and skills to support their learning across the curriculum. To provide this framework, you may want to teach certain grammatical elements in a systematic way. The assessment checklists provided in each level of **Good Grammar!** indicate the grammatical elements that students should understand by the end of each level. The checklists can be used to program your systematic teaching, and to record children's achievements.

Incidental teaching

Incidental teaching is an important strategy to use to help children build on prior learning and develop their understanding of grammar in context. A grammar lesson might therefore stem from the context of different texts children are reading and writing, or from the need to deal with a specific problem individual children or groups of children are experiencing in their own writing. To teach at this point of need, simply dip into **Good Grammar!** and find the appropriate information, strategies or worksheets for your children.

Assessment

To be successful, any grammar program must be accompanied by regular assessment. The methods used may differ from teacher to teacher but should encompass the following points.

For each student, assessment should:

(a) record clearly the progress being made;
(b) indicate the future steps being planned for reinforcement and extension;
(c) indicate specific areas of difficulty and possible remediation;
(d) use various strategies to determine whether an outcome has been achieved;
(e) be a relevant and careful measurement of the stage of grammar development;
(f) provide clear and precise suggestions to parents as to how they may best assist at home;
(g) provide clear and precise information to teachers.

Assessment Checklist

Name _____ Term

Parts of Speech

	1	2	3	4
Understands, identifies and uses correctly:				
different types of nouns, including abstract				
action, saying, thinking, and being and having verbs				
tense				
subject/verb agreement				
different types of adjectives				
a variety of adverbs				
degrees of comparison				
definite and indefinite articles				
prepositions as place words				
personal, possessive and relative pronouns				
conjunctions and connecting words				

Sentences

	1	2	3	4
Identifies:				
subject, verb and object				
phrases and clauses				
dependency of one clause on another				
Identifies and writes:				
simple, compound and complex sentences				
direct speech and indirect speech				
adverbial phrases and adjectival phrases				

Punctuation

	1	2	3	4
capital letters				
full stops, question marks				
commas, semicolons, colons, dash				
apostrophes				
question marks in direct speech				

Comments

Areas of strength _____

Areas of difficulty _____

Steps being undertaken to reinforce areas of difficulty or extend grammar skills

3

© P. Clutterbuck, Good Grammar! Book 3. This page may be reproduced for classroom use.

Parts of Speech

Every name is called a **noun**,
As *fence* and *flower*, *street* and *town*;

In place of noun the **pronoun** stands,
As *he* and *she* can raise their hands;

The **adjective** describes a thing,
As *magic* wand and *twisted* string;

The **verb** means action, something done—
To *read* and *write*, to *jump* and *run*;

How things are done the **adverbs** tell,
As *quickly, slowly, badly, well*;

The **preposition** shows the place,
As *in* the street or *at* the base;

Conjunctions join, in many ways,
Sentences, words, *or* phrase *and* phrase.

anonymous

© P. Clutterbuck, Good Grammar! Book 3. This page may be reproduced for classroom use.

Nouns

Introduction

Upper Primary children should be familiar with the following functions of a noun.

(a) Nouns are the **names** of things around us. Nouns that are used to name general things (rather than a particular person or thing) are called **common nouns**. Examples:

dog   *table*   *car*   *bottle*

(b) Some nouns are the names of particular or special people or things. These are called **proper nouns** and are written with a capital letter at the beginning. Examples:

Michael Jackson stayed at the Hilton Hotel in Adelaide last July.

(c) Some nouns are the names we use for collections of things. These are called **collective nouns.** Examples:

a *flock* of birds   a *herd* of cattle   a *bunch* of grapes
a *smack* of jellyfish   a *siege* of bears   a *murder* of ravens
an *army* of frogs   a *charm* of finches   a *pod* of dolphins

Other collective nouns name a number of different things in the same class. Examples:

fruit   *tools*   *luggage*   *birds*

Children often have difficulty deciding whether a collective noun is singular or plural.

- Words that represent a number of different things in the same group always take a single verb. Examples:

    furniture is   *luggage is*   *linen is*

- Words that have a plural meaning but no plural form take a plural verb. Examples:

    people are   *police are*

- Other collective nouns can take a plural verb if the context emphasis is on a group of individuals. However the singular is preferred. Examples:

    The crowd is cheering.
    Parliament is sitting.
    The crew is ready.
    The Olympic Games are in Sydney.

(d) Nouns can be **singular** or **plural**. The relevant plural constructions at this level are:

- Many plurals are made by simply adding *-s*. Examples:
    dog/dogs   girl/girls
- If the noun ends in *-s*, *-sh*, *-ch* or *-x*, make the plural by adding *-es*. Examples:
    bus/buses   bush/bushes   church/churches   fox/foxes
- If the noun ends in a *-y* before which there is a consonant, make the plural by changing *-y* to *-i* and adding *-es* . Examples:
    fairy/fairies   city/cities
- If the noun ends in *-y* before which there is a vowel, (a, e, i, o, u) make the plural by simply adding *-s*. Examples:
    monkey/monkeys   toy/toys
- If the noun ends in *-f*, change the *-f* to *-v* and add *-es*. Examples:
    loaf/loaves   leaf/leaves
    However some simply add *-s*. Examples:
    roof/roofs   chief/chiefs
- Some nouns have an irregular plural. Examples:
    foot/feet   goose/geese   man/men   child/children

(e) **Possessive nouns** are especially difficult for children at this level to grasp.

- The possessive of a singular noun is formed by adding an apostrophe and *-s* at the end of the word. No letters are changed or left off the original word. Examples:
    the *boy's* dog (the boy owns a dog)
    the *lady's* car (the lady owns a car)
- The possessive of a plural noun ending in *-s* is formed by adding an *apostrophe*. Examples:
    horses/*horses'* manes   ladies/*ladies'* cars
- The possessive of a plural noun not ending in *-s* is formed by adding an *apostrophe* and *-s*. Examples:
    children/*children's*   men/*men's*

(f) **Terms of address** are the nouns we use when we refer to or address certain people. Examples:
    Mr Jones *Ms* Smith   *Doctor* Smith   *Captain* Peters

(g) An **abstract noun** is the name of something that can't be recognised by the five senses—you can't touch, taste, hear, smell or see it—it can only be recognised by the mind. Examples:

courage	*misery*	*delight*	*fear*
excitement	*distress*	*hope*	*possibility*

Children should also be introduced to the relationship of nouns to words such as verbs (words that tell what the noun is doing), adjectives (words that describe the noun) and pronouns (words that take the place of a noun).

Teaching Strategies

Alphabet game
Challenge children to write a common noun for every letter of the alphabet. These could be related to a particular topic or theme, for example, the Earth, cities or endangered species. Make the challenge more exciting by adding a time limit. They could then repeat the activity with proper nouns.

Labels
Have children draw a diagram, for example a car, bicycle or horse, and then add labels.

Lists
Have children make lists of nouns, such as: Things I Need to Take on the School Camp or Things I Might See in the City.

Mystery nouns
Children can describe a mystery object and challenge classmates to guess what it is.
I am a sphere.
I am made of glass.
You play games with me.
(marble)

Puzzles
Have children make anagram or jumbled letter puzzles for their classmates to solve.
flow=wolf
arrtoc (vegetable)=carrot

Cloze

Create cloze exercises by selecting an extract from a story and blotting out the nouns. Have children add a noun that maintains the context of the story.

Proper noun match

Read aloud a list of common nouns. Have children supply a proper noun for each.
planet/Venus
country/Cuba
river/Murrumbidgee

Lots of

Read aloud a sentence which includes the words 'lots of'. Have children suggest a suitable collective noun.
I saw lots of birds.
I saw lots of cars.

Unusual collections

Encourage children to explore collective nouns that are not so well known. Encyclopaedias and dictionaries will assist them.

Made-up collections

After discussing common collective nouns with children (a flock of birds, a herd of cattle) have them make up their own imaginary collective nouns that they feel would suit a group of creatures.
a slither of snakes   *a hop of frogs*
a gathering of goannas   *a trumpet of elephants*

Abstract mime

Write abstract nouns on slips of paper and place the papers in a hat. Allow children to take turns to pick a paper from the hat and mime the abstract noun. The rest of the class must guess the abstract noun.
happiness
sadness
anger
kindness

Abstract opposites

Have children provide the opposite words for abstract nouns you read aloud.
love/hate
beauty/ugliness

WORD BANK

Common Nouns

aeroplane	country	maid	saddle
aunt	creek	match	seat
basket	daughter	money	shirt
bath	dentist	monkey	shoulder
blanket	doctor	motor	soup
blood	donkey	mum	stairs
body	earth	music	stream
bottle	engine	needle	sugar
breath	fairy	neighbour	tail
bridge	flames	nephew	teacher
bucket	floor	newspaper	tears
button	holiday	niece	toast
cabin	honey	ocean	tomatoes
camel	husband	pencil	tunnel
captain	island	person	valley
castle	jelly	piano	village
chair	knee	picnic	whale
chalk	knife	potatoes	wheat
cliff	ladder	pupil	women
coach	lamb	rooster	

© P. Clutterbuck, Good Grammar! Book 3. This page may be reproduced for classroom use.

WORD BANK

NOUNS

Proper Nouns

Aunty Tanya
the Big Banana
Captain Cook
Christmas
Christmas Day
Doctor Smith
Easter
Mum
Norfolk Island
the Sydney Opera House

Collective Nouns

army	family
band	flotilla
bunch	forest
class	gang
club	herd
committee	litter
congregation	pack
convoy	police
crew	swarm
	team

Abstract Nouns

anger	distress	honour	love
beauty	excitement	hope	misery
consideration	fear	idea	pity
courage	friendship	imagination	pleasure
danger	fun	joy	possibility
delight	gladness	kindness	prettiness
despair	greed	laughter	sadness
dismay	happiness	loneliness	shame

© P. Clutterbuck, Good Grammar! Book 3. This page may be reproduced for classroom use.

Common Nouns

Name _____   **Grammar BLM** 1

Nouns that are used to name general things are called common nouns.

1. Sort the nouns in the box under the headings below.

knees	yachting	caviar	biscuits	steak
bacon	stomach	football	polo	beanie
jacket	veins	anorak skull	hockey	trouser

Clothing   Body   Food   Sport

_____   _____   _____   _____

_____   _____   _____   _____

_____   _____   _____   _____

_____   _____   _____   _____

2. Write the word from the box that names each group of things.

a. cassowary, emu, plover   _____

b. stool, desk, table   _____

c. badminton, lacrosse, soccer   _____

d. carriage, coach, car   _____

e. orchid, daisy, pansy   _____

f. currants, cherries, apricots _____

g. herring, flounder, cod   _____

h. spaniels, terriers, poodles   _____

sports
flowers
birds
dogs
furniture
fish
vehicles
fruit

3. Circle the noun in each row that is out of place.

a. butterfly grasshopper thistle wasp   d. lettuce   apricot carrot   onion

b. walrus palm olive maple   e. attic   cellar   kitchen stomach

c. panther lion tiger zebra   f. planet   doctor   nurse   surgeon

11

© P. Clutterbuck, Good Grammar! Book 3. This page may be reproduced for classroom use.

Common Nouns

Nouns that are used to name general things are called common nouns.

1. Find the nouns in the grid. Write each one beside its meaning.

r	t	t	r	o	u	t	b
a	i	p	e	a	c	h	r
v	g	o	n	i	o	n	a
e	e	p	a	n	s	y	s
n	r	l	o	u	s	e	s
s	k	u	l	l	x	z	p
b	r	e	a	d	y	t	v

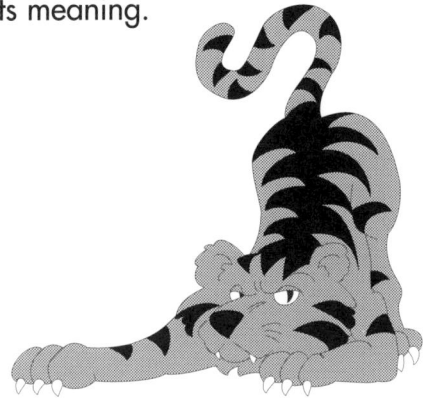

a. body part _____
b. insect _____
c. fruit _____
d. fish _____
e. bird _____

f. food _____
g. metal _____
h. flower _____
i. vegetable _____
j. large cat _____

2. Colour the boxes that contain a noun.

barrel	falcon	bugle	leather	vinegar
happy	silly	orchid	sofa	canal
eel	pitcher	chewing	dirty	tall
old	silk	hamper	ferret	envelope

3. Choose 5 nouns from question 2. Write a sentence using each one.

a. _____

b. _____

c. _____

d. _____

e. _____

12

© P. Clutterbuck, Good Grammar! Book 3. This page may be reproduced for classroom use.

Collective Nouns

Collective nouns are the names we use for collections of things.

1. Use a collective noun from the box to fill each space.

> brood   fleet   library   litter   tuft   flight   batch   bunch

a. a_____ of aircraft

b. a_____ of cakes

c. a_____ of grass

d. a_____ of grapes

e. a_____ of ships

f. a_____ of puppies

g. a_____ of chickens

h. a_____ of books

2. Add a collective noun from the box to complete each sentence.

> bouquet   hail   gaggle   pride   staff   plague

a. On our farm we have a _____ geese.

b. The gangster dropped in a _____ of bullets.

c. The bride carried a _____ of flowers.

d. A _____ of grasshoppers devoured the lawn.

e. A _____ of lions dozed under the trees.

f. My mum's company has a large _____ .

3. Add a collective noun of your own on each line below.

a. a _____ of footballers

b. a _____ of eggs

c. a _____ of sheep

d. a _____ of sailors

e. a _____ of hay

f. a _____ of wool

g. a _____ of trees

h. a _____ of bananas

© P. Clutterbuck, Good Grammar! Book 3. This page may be reproduced for classroom use.

Proper Nouns

Name _____ **Grammar BLM** **4**

Proper nouns are the names of particular people, places or things. They are written with a capital letter at the beginning.

1. Write the proper noun from the box beside the matching common noun below.

> September   Nile   Tuesday   Matthew Flinders   Cairns   Japan

a. country _____
b. month _____
c. explorer _____

d. river _____
e. day _____
f. city _____

2. Use the proper nouns in the box to complete the story.

> Bass Strait   Vanessa   Monday   Portland   April
> Good Friday   Tony   Victoria Tasmania   Seahawk

On _____ the eighth of _____ two students, a girl named _____ and a boy named _____ , left the seaside city of _____ in _____ to sail a yacht named _____ across _____ _____ to _____ . They arrived safely on _____ _____ , much to the relief of their parents.

3. Write the word from the box that names each group of proper nouns.

> months
> oceans
> planets
> countries
> states
> mountains

a. Chile, Canada, England _____
b. June, August, July _____
c. Saturn, Uranus, Neptune _____
d. Everest, Kosciuzko, Kilimanjaro _____
e. Pacific, Atlantic, Indian _____
f. Queensland, Western Australia, Victoria _____

© P. Clutterbuck, Good Grammar! Book 3. This page may be reproduced for classroom use.

Plural Nouns

Name _____ **Grammar BLM** **5**

Singular nouns refer to one person, place or thing. Plural nouns refer to more than one person, place or thing.

1. Write the plural of the word in brackets. Hint! If there is a vowel before the *y*, add *s*. If there is a consonant before the *y*, change the *y* to *i* and add *es*.

a. All the children in our school were given _____ . (diary)

b. There are lots of large _____ in Australia. (city)

c. The _____ were making a lot of noise. (turkey)

d. This supermarket has over five hundred_____. (trolley)

e. We ate all the _____ on the tree. (cherry)

f. Lots of _____ gathered around the rotten food. (fly)

2. Write the plural of each word. Hint! For some words that end in *f*, change the *f* to *v* and add *es*. For others, simply add *s*.

a. loaf _____   e. leaf   _____

b. chief _____   f. handkerchief _____

c. knife _____   g. thief   _____

d. half _____   h. wolf   _____

3. Write the plural of the word in brackets.

a. The two _____ decided to end the war. (army)

b. They read the story 'Snow White and the Seven _____'. (Dwarf)

c. When the box was dropped, all the _____ broke. (glass)

d. At the zoo we saw lots of _____. (monkey)

e. Several_____ were needed to pull the wagon. (ox)

f. The_____ left their coats on the bed. (lady)

Plural Nouns

Singular nouns refer to one person, place or thing. Plural nouns refer to more than one person, place or thing.

1. Write the plural of the word in brackets. Hint! Most nouns form the plural by adding *s*. Those that end in *ch, sh, s* or *x* add *es*.

a. There are over seven _____ in our town. (**church**)

b. There are lots of _____ growing in the playground. (**tree**)

c. The frightened dog hid between the two _____ . (**bush**)

d. Jan put all the _____ on the table. (**box**)

e. My brother ate three _____ for lunch. (**peach**)

f. The six school _____ were in a line. (**bus**)

2. Write the plural of each of the following words. Hint! They are all irregular.

a. goose _____   e. tooth _____

b. man _____   f. woman _____

c. foot _____   g. child _____

d. house _____   h. mouse _____

3. Write the plural of the word in brackets. Hint! Some nouns that end in *o* add *es* to make the plural. Others simply add *s*.

a. We planted _____ in the garden. (**potato**)

b. On our holiday, Kyle took lots of _____ . (**photo**)

c. South America has many _____ . (**volcano**)

d. Hundreds of _____ damaged the wheat crop. (**kangaroo**)

e. The brave _____ were all given medals. (**hero**)

f. I sliced the three _____ to make a salad. (**tomato**)

16

© P. Clutterbuck, Good Grammar! Book 3. This page may be reproduced for classroom use.

Forming Nouns

Nouns can be formed from other parts of speech.

1. Complete the sentence by making a noun from the verb in brackets.

a. We placed an _____ in the newspaper. (**advertise**)

b. The _____ took place in a nearby church. (**marry**)

c. Our teacher asked for our complete _____ . (**attend**)

d. Ian's _____ has been much better this term. (**behave**)

e. They had to make an important _____ . (**decide**)

f. The teacher gave us a lot of _____ . (**encourage**)

2. Complete the sentence by making a noun from the adjective in brackets.

a. It was with great _____ we said goodbye. (**sad**)

b. The firefighter was awarded for her _____ . (**brave**)

c. We sat in the coolness of the _____ . (**shade**)

d. There was a lot of _____ between the two teams. (**bitter**)

e. We gasped at the _____ of the mountains. (**beautiful**)

f. We were not sure what _____ he was suffering from. (**sick**)

3. Make nouns from each of the words below.

a. punish   a severe _____

b. invent   a clever _____

c. friendly   a good _____

d. appear   an untidy _____

e. weigh   a heavy _____

f. lose   a sad _____

© P. Clutterbuck, Good Grammar! Book 3. This page may be reproduced for classroom use.

Possessive Nouns

Name _____ Grammar BLM **8**

**An apostrophe is used to show possession
(that something belongs to something or someone).**
- **For a singular noun add an *apostrophe* and *s* at the end of the word.**
  the horse's mane
  the child's toys
- **For a plural noun add an *apostrophe* if the word ends in *s***
  the horses' manes
  or an *apostrophe* s if the word does not end in *s*
  the children's toys.

1. Rewrite the following to show possession.

a. the dress of the girl _____

b. the stripes of the tiger _____

c. the pencil of the boy _____

d. the handbags of the lady _____

e. the leaves of the tree _____

f. the petals of the flower _____

g. the antics of the clown _____

h. the uniform of the police officer _____

2. Now rewrite the following to show possession.

a. the dresses of the girls _____

b. the ears of the donkeys _____

c. the books of the men _____

d. the saddles of the horses _____

e. the houses of the women _____

f. the pencils of the boys _____

g. the nests of the birds _____

h. the ship of the sailors _____

18

© P. Clutterbuck, Good Grammar! Book 3. This page may be reproduced for classroom use.

Abstract Nouns

Name _____ Grammar BLM 9

An abstract noun is the name of something that can't be recognised by the five senses. You can't touch, taste, hear, smell or see it—it can only be recognised by the mind.

1. Add an abstract noun from the box to fill each space.

> excitement   fun   pain   health   length   happiness   care   wealth

a. We had lots of _____ at the show.

b. After he fell over Tom had a _____ in his leg.

c. Although he has been ill, he is in good _____ now.

d. There was a lot of _____ when the mouse escaped in the classroom.

e. I am not sure of the _____ of this rope.

f. Mr Richman thinks that _____ is important.

g. The genie said that I would have health, wealth and _____ .

h. Tim took a lot of _____ with his work.

2. Find the abstract nouns in this grid. Write them on the lines.

s	a	d	n	e	s	s
g	s	o	r	r	o	w
r	g	r	i	e	f	g
e	l	p	a	i	n	l
e	o	f	e	a	r	e
d	v	j	o	y	x	e
x	e	a	n	g	e	r

_____   _____

_____   _____

_____   _____

_____   _____

_____   _____

3. Write an abstract noun to suit each situation. Compare your answers with those of a friend.

a. Your younger brother scribbles all over your new book. _____

b. You teacher tells you there is no school next week. _____

c. You have played sport all day. _____

d. A poisonous spider lands on your arm. _____

© P. Clutterbuck, Good Grammar! Book 3. This page may be reproduced for classroom use.

Verbs

Introduction

Upper Primary children should understand the following types of verbs and their uses.

(a) **Action verbs** are words that express a concrete action. They are common in spoken language and in the writing of young children. Examples:

> *work   run   sit   eat   jump*

(b) **Saying verbs** express a spoken action. Examples:

> *talk   tell   said   suggested   yelled*

(c) Some verbs do not express a concrete action—they express actions that happen mentally, such as feelings, ideas, thoughts or attitudes. These can be called **thinking and feeling verbs**. They are common in arguments, narratives and descriptions (but not scientific descriptions, which are objective). Examples:

> I *like* Sam.   Katy *believed* the story.
> I *see* the rabbit.   I *think* people should recycle.

(d) Some verbs tell us about what things are and what they have. These are **being and having verbs**. They are common in all kinds of descriptions. Examples:

> Ben *is* a good swimmer.   Ali *has* the answer.   They *are* here.
> (*Is, are, has* and *have* can also act as auxiliaries, or helping verbs, for doing, thinking and feeling verbs. Example: Ben *is* swimming.)

Verbs can be **finite** or **non-finite**.

(a) **Finite** verbs have a subject. Example:

> *The dog bit my leg.*

The verb is *bit*. To find the subject ask "Who or what bit?". In this case there is an answer—*the dog*—so there is a subject.
Finite verbs can also stand alone without a helping verb. For a sentence to be complete it must have a finite verb.

(b) **Non-finite verbs** cannot stand alone. Example:

> *to go* to the dance

Non-finite verbs can be infinitives or participles.

- The infinitive usually consists of a verb before which is the word *to*. Examples:

> *to jump*   *to hop*

Often the *to* is not written or spoken. Examples:

> Fred made me *do* this.   Let me *go* with Sam.

- **Participles** are parts of verbs. When they are used with helping verbs (auxiliaries), they form complete verbs. Example:

  Jack is *running* across the lawn.

  The helping verb is *is* and the present participle is *running*.

  Participles can be present or past. Examples:

  | present | *swimming* | *skipping* | *hopping* |
  | past | *swum* | *skipped* | *hopped* |

  Note that a participle must never be used on its own as a verb.

Correct	**Incorrect**
I have done.	I done.
I have seen.	I seen.

Verbs do not only express actions; they also tell us the time of the action. The **tense** of a verb tells us when the action is, was, or will be carried out.

The three tenses are past, present and future.

(a) **Present tense** refers to actions that are happening now, at this moment. Example:

  I *like* the chocolate flavour.

(b) **Past tense** refers to actions that happened in the past, a few seconds ago or years ago. Example:

  I *liked* the chocolate flavour.

  Don't confuse the past tense with the past participle. Remember, the past participle always has a helping verb. Example:

  | Past tense | I *rang*. |
  | Past participle | I *have rung*. |

(c) **Future tense** refers to actions which will happen in the future, in a few seconds or in a few years. Example:

  She *will like* the chocolate flavour.

There are different forms of the present, past and future tenses.

(a) The examples above are in the **simple** or **indefinite form**.

(b) The other main form that Upper Primary children should be aware of is the **continuous form**. It refers to an action that is, was or will be continuing.

Present continuous tense	He *is walking* along the road.
Past continuous tense	He *was walking* along the road.
Future continuous tense	He *will be walking* along the road.

Most verbs form their tenses in a regular way according to the following table.

REGULAR VERBS		
Present Tense	**Past Tense**	**Past Participle**
I watch	I watched	(I have) watched
He plays	He played	(He has) played
They use	They used	(They have) used

Irregular verbs do not simply add *-ed* to form the past tense. The verb itself changes—and these changes have to be learned. (A good dictionary will list these changes.)

A verb can be in the **active** or the **passive voice**. The voice of the verb tells whether the subject is doing the action (active voice) or whether something is being done to the subject (passive voice). When the passive voice is used the verb includes an auxiliary (helping verb) and a participle (main verb). Examples:

Active voice   Katy *read* the book.
Passive voice   The book *was read* by Katy.

Active voice is more direct, and usually shorter and easier to read than passive voice. Passive voice is often used in reports and explanations to neutralise events, and in public notices to make them less hostile. Examples:

Active voice   Do not *put* your feet on the seats!
Passive voice   Feet must not be *put* on the seats.

Children at this level should be able to talk about **subject/verb agreement** in a sentence. They are generally quick to identify times when the verb does not agree with the subject in number.

- If the subject is plural (more than one), a plural verb is required. Examples:
    The *boys are coming* down the road.
    The *girls like* ice-cream.
- If a subject is singular, a singular verb is required. Examples:
    The *boy is coming* down the road.
    The *girl likes* ice-cream.
- If there is more than one subject joined by *and*, a plural verb is required. Example:
    Here *come* the *bride* and *groom*.
- Collective nouns usually take a singular verb. See the chapter on nouns for more information.

Teaching Strategies

Puzzle verbs

On the chalkboard write the first letter of a verb and then a dash for each remaining letter. Tell the class what the verb means. Have volunteers come out and add the missing letters.

g _ _ _ _ _   *to run like a horse*
w _ _ _   *to cry*

Verb lists

Spend time encouraging students to seek out and use the most suitable verb at all times. This can be done by simple exercises on the chalkboard.
The frightened rabbit ran to its hole.
Have children replace *ran* with more effective verbs.
bolted   hopped   shot   leaped

Charades

Have children act out roles while others guess what they are doing.
You are drying the dishes.

Mixed-up verbs

Have children add suitable verbs to given nouns.
Dogs bark. Cats purr.
They can then mix them up in a humorous way and create cartoons.
Fish bark.   Dogs fly.

Make it active

Have children identify verbs in a sentence and state whether they are in the active or passive voice.
Tom read the newspaper.
The newspaper was read by Tom.
Have children change sentences from the passive to the active voice.

In the past

Provide plenty of practice for children in the use of the past tense and past participles, especially of irregular verbs. These can be short oral activities.
I drive my car —but yesterday I _____ my car.
I have _____ my car.

I think . . .

Encourage each child to orally state their opinions on certain topics. Remind them to use thinking and feeling verbs.
I believe that . . .
It seems that . . .
As children become more confident, conduct panel games or simple debates.

WORD BANK

VERBS

Irregular Verbs

Present Tense	Past Tense	Past Participle
am	was	been
bear	bore	borne
beat	beat	beaten
become	became	become
begin	began	begun
bite	bit	bitten
bleed	bled	bled
blow	blew	blown
break	broke	broken
bring	brought	brought
broadcast	broadcast	broadcast
build	built	built
burst	burst	burst
buy	bought	bought
catch	caught	caught
choose	chose	chosen
come	came	come
creep	crept	crept
deal	dealt	dealt
do	did	done
draw	drew	drawn
drink	drank	drunk
drive	drove	driven
drown	drowned	drowned
eat	ate	eaten
fall	fell	fallen
feel	felt	felt
fight	fought	fought
flee	fled	fled
fly	flew	flown
forget	forgot	forgotten
forsake	forsook	forsake
freeze	froze	frozen
give	gave	given
go	went	gone
grow	grew	grown
hang (article)	hung	hung
hang (person)	hanged	hanged
hide	hid	hidden
hold	held	held
hurt	hurt	hurt

24

© P. Clutterbuck, Good Grammar! Book 3. This page may be reproduced for classroom use.

Irregular Verbs

Present Tense	Past Tense	Past Participle
kneel	knelt	knelt
know	knew	known
lay	laid	laid
leave	left	left
lie	lay	lain
mow	mowed	mown
ride	rode	ridden
ring	rang	rung
rise	rose	risen
run	ran	run
saw (wood)	sawed	sawn
see	saw	seen
seek	sought	sought
shake	shook	shaken
show	showed	shown
sing	sang	sung
sink	sank	sunk
slay	slew	slain
speak	spoke	spoken
spring	sprang	sprung
steal	stole	stolen
strike	struck	struck
swear	swore	sworn
swell	swelled	swollen
swim	swam	swum
take	took	taken
teach	taught	taught
tear	tore	torn
think	thought	thought
throw	threw	thrown
tread	trod	trodden
wear	wore	worn
weave	wove	woven
wind	wound	wound
wring	wrung	wrung
write	wrote	written

© P. Clutterbuck, Good Grammar! Book 3. This page may be reproduced for classroom use.

WORD BANK

VERBS

Action Verbs

bounce
build
dawdle
fight
hurtle
kick
knock
meander
saunter
scatter
shatter
shuffle
slither
squeeze
stagger
struggle
stumble
wriggle

Saying Verbs

bellowed
cheered
chuckled
exclaimed
giggled
growled
howled
joked
laughed
moaned
roared
shouted
shrieked
sighed
snarled
sniggered
sobbed
squealed
stormed
wailed

Thinking and Feeling Verbs

believe
dislike
doubt
feel
know
like
prefer
seem
suppose
think
understand
wonder

Being and Having Verbs

am
are
had
has
have
is
was
were

© P. Clutterbuck, Good Grammar! Book 3. This page may be reproduced for classroom use.

Verbs

Action verbs express an action we can see.
For example: *work, run, sit.*

1. Circle the action verb in each sentence.
a. The dog bit the postman.
b. Ian listened carefully.
c. The teacher tapped the table with his ruler.
d. Susan read a book about dinosaurs.
e. The dog ate the old bone.
f. We wandered through the rainforest.

2. Use a verb from the box to fill each space.

> pounced   scowled   searched   pruned   wiped   gushed

a. When we turned the tap the water_____ out.
b. The angry lady_____ at me.
c. The hungry cat_____ on the mouse.
d. After he finished the ice-cream he_____ his face.
e. The farmer _____ the fruit trees.
f. We_____ everywhere but could not find the missing watch.

3. What does each do?

> leaps   gambols   gallops   slithers
> scampers   soars   waddles   struts

a. A snake _____ .
b. A horse_____ .
c. A lamb_____ .
d. A frog _____ .
e. A rooster_____ .
f. A duck _____ .
g. An eagle _____ .
h. A mouse _____ .

© P. Clutterbuck, Good Grammar! Book 3. This page may be reproduced for classroom use.

Verbs

Action verbs express an action we can see.
For example: *work, run, sit.*

1. Circle the action verb in each sentence.
   a. The builders constructed the new home.
   b. We grilled the sausages on the barbecue.
   c. Heavy rain fell on the roof last night.
   d. The mechanic removed the nuts from the bolts.
   e. Sally wrote a letter to her friend.
   f. The acrobats performed some amazing stunts.

2. Use a verb from the box to fill each space.

quench	comb	burst	throw	draw	obey

   a. to _____ a picture   d. to _____ your thirst

   b. to _____ an order   e. to _____ your hair

   c. to _____ a ball   f. to _____ a balloon

3. Add an action verb of your own to complete each sentence. Then think of a different action verb to give the sentence a different meaning.

   a. The cat _____ its tail.   The cat _____ its tail.

   b. The ball _____ the window.   The ball _____ the window.

   c. Dad _____ the dishes.   Dad _____ the dishes.

   d. The car _____ on the greasy road.   The car _____ on the greasy road.

28

© P. Clutterbuck, Good Grammar! Book 3. This page may be reproduced for classroom use.

Verbs

Name _____ **Grammar BLM** **12**

Action verbs express an action we can see.
For example: _work, run, sit._

1. Sort the action verbs under the headings.

catching	studying	batting	browsing
roasting	fielding	cleaning	cooking
researching	peeling	reading	bowling

at a cricket match   in the library   in the kitchen

_____   _____   _____

_____   _____   _____

_____   _____   _____

_____   _____   _____

2. Circle the action verb in the brackets.

a. The dog went straight out to (**bury** **berry**) the bone.

b. They tried to (**pier** **peer**) through the curtains.

c. The rocket (**mist** **missed**) its target.

d. It is rude to (**stair** **stare**) at other people.

e. Water supplies began to (**lessen** **lesson**) during the drought.

3. Unjumble the letters in brackets and write the action verb in the space.

a. Tomorrow the chickens should _____ from the eggs. (**ahtch**)

b. I was lucky the wasp did not _____ me. (**ingst**)

c. It is my job to _____ the clothes. (**awsh**)

d. Be careful your little brother does not _____ that toy. (**wsallow**)

e. I saw the dog _____ the fence. (**umjp**)

29

© P. Clutterbuck, Good Grammar! Book 3. This page may be reproduced for classroom use.

Verbs

Saying verbs express a spoken action.
For example: *talk, tell, said.*

1. Circle the saying verb in each sentence.
a. Sally talked to the new boy.
b. Tom yelled at the dog that was eating his pie.
c. "I will be late," said Ben.
d. The children chatted for a long time before going to sleep.
e. The teacher asked the class to get back to work.
f. They screamed when the big dipper suddenly dropped back to Earth.

2. Add a saying verb of your own to each sentence.
a. The boy _____ as he ran down the street.
b. She _____ as she slipped on the wet floor.
c. Year Six _____ when they were told they had raised the
    most money.
d. The children _____ as they slid down the water slide.
e. The cat _____ as she ran towards her dish of food.
f. The angry mother _____, "Tidy up your room!"

3. What noise does each make?

> grunts   trumpets   chirps   bellows
> brays   bleats   screeches   gobbles

a. a lamb _____   e. a pig _____
b. a turkey _____   f. an elephant _____
c. a parrot _____   g. a sparrow _____
d. a donkey _____   h. a bull _____

© P. Clutterbuck, Good Grammar! Book 3. This page may be reproduced for classroom use.

Verbs

Name _____ Grammar BLM **14**

Thinking verbs express actions that happen mentally, such as feelings, ideas, thoughts or attitudes. For example: I *like* Sam.

1. Circle the thinking verb in each sentence.
a. I believed the story.
b. I think people should recycle.
c. I wondered what would happen next.
d. Tom thought about it for a while.
e. I understand what you mean.
f. Did you enjoy the movie?

2. Change the noun in brackets to a thinking verb.

a. I am _____ . (anger)

b. The principal was_____ by the graffiti. (**sadness**)

c. I was_____ by the story. (**amazement**)

d. The new boy_____about his achievements. (**boastfulness**)

e. I_____ that we should leave at four o'clock. (**agreement**)

f. I_____ being forced to eat my vegetables. (**hatred**)

3. Write your thoughts and feelings on an issue that is important to you. Then circle all the thinking and feeling verbs you have used.

_____

_____

_____

_____

_____

_____

© P. Clutterbuck, Good Grammar! Book 3. This page may be reproduced for classroom use.

Verbs

Being and having verbs tell us about what things are and what they have. For example: Ben *is* a good swimmer.
Being and having verbs are sometimes confused with words acting as auxiliaries (or helping verbs) for doing, saying and thinking verbs.
For example: Ben *is swimming*.

1. Circle the being or having verb in each sentence.
a. Max has a bad cold.
b. Ali is the best speller.
c. The books are here.
d. Nick was there a minute ago.
e. I am the captain of the team.
f. I have the string.

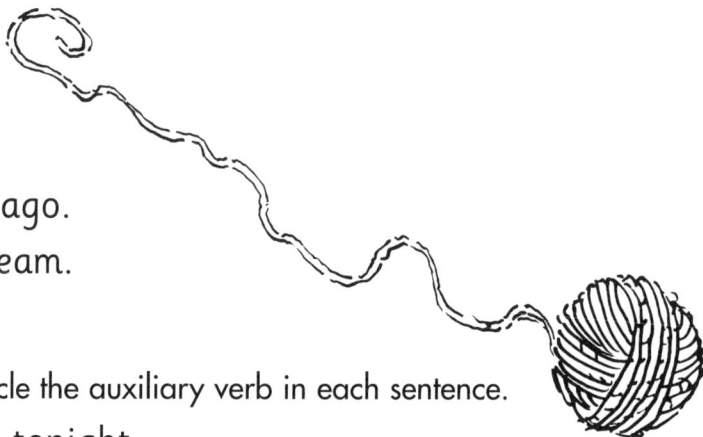

2. Underline the main verb and circle the auxiliary verb in each sentence.
a. I am going to the movies tonight.
b. Mum is painting the house this weekend.
c. The teacher was helping us.
d. Tom will run in the race.
e. Our class has read that book.
f. I have seen a shooting star.

3. Use three of the being and having verbs from question 1 in sentences of your own.

_____

_____

_____

4. Use three of the verb groups (auxiliary verb plus main verb) from question 2 in sentences of your own.

_____

_____

_____

© P. Clutterbuck, Good Grammar! Book 3. This page may be reproduced for classroom use.

Verb Tense

Name _____ Grammar BLM **16**

The tense of a verb tells us when the action is, was, or will be carried out. Present tense refers to actions that are happening now, at this moment. Past tense refers to actions that happened in the past, a few seconds ago or years ago. Future tense refers to actions that will happen in the future, in a few seconds or in a few years.

Present tense: She *likes* the chocolate flavour.
Past tense: She *liked* the chocolate flavour.
Future tense: She *will like* the chocolate flavour.

1. Change each of the words in the box to the past tense verb. Then use the past tense verbs to complete the sentences. Hint! Some words add *-ed* to make the past tense.

> delight__   defeat__   bark__   thank__   start__   walk__

a. I _____ the teacher for helping me throughout the year.
b. The dog_____ loudly at the stranger.
c. Our football team_____ the other team ten goals to three.
d. I was _____ when I was told I had won the prize.
e. We_____ over three kilometres to the nearest house.
f. The concert_____ right on time.

2. Change each of the words in the box to the past tense verb. Then use the past tense verbs to complete the sentences. Hint! If the word ends in *-e*, add *-d* to make the past tense.

> whistle__   refuse__   waste__   describe__   capture__   continue__

a. The hunters _____ the leopard in the net.
b. The soldier_____ to obey the orders of her sergeant.
c. The children_____ a lot of good food on the camp.
d. He _____ loudly to call his dog.
e. The witness _____ the thief to the police officer.
f. Although her leg had hurt badly Freya_____ the race.

33

© P. Clutterbuck, Good Grammar! Book 3. This page may be reproduced for classroom use.

Verb Tense

The tense of a verb tells us when the action is, was, or will be carried out. Present tense refers to actions that are happening now, at this moment. Past tense refers to actions that happened in the past, a few seconds ago or years ago. Future tense refers to actions that will happen in the future, in a few seconds or in a few years.

Present tense: She *likes* the chocolate flavour.
Past tense: She *liked* the chocolate flavour.
Future tense: She *will like* the chocolate flavour.

1. Write the past tense verbs on the lines. Hint! If the word ends in -*y*, change the -*y* to -*i* and add -*ed* to make the past tense.

a. study _____
b. deny _____
c. multiply _____
d. bury _____

e. terrify _____
f. tidy _____
g. copy _____
h. hurry _____

2. Use the past tense verbs from question 1 to complete the sentences.

a. The dog _____ its bone in the garden.
b. When I _____ two by four I got eight.
c. The thief _____ stealing the jewels.
d. Sally _____ hard to pass her spelling test.
e. The savage dog _____ the young child.
f. I _____ up the lounge room for my mother.
g. Mike _____ the answers from Peter.
h. Joanne _____ to school because she thought she was late.

© P. Clutterbuck, Good Grammar! Book 3. This page may be reproduced for classroom use.

Verb Tense

The tense of a verb tells us when the action is, was, or will be carried out. Present tense refers to actions that are happening now, at this moment. Past tense refers to actions that happened in the past, a few seconds ago or years ago. Future tense refers to actions that will happen in the future, in a few seconds or in a few years.

Present tense: She *likes* the chocolate flavour.

Past tense: She *liked* the chocolate flavour.

Future tense: She *will like* the chocolate flavour.

1. Complete the sentences by writing the past tense of the verb in brackets Hint! Some verbs form the past tense by doubling the final letter and adding -ed.

   a. The car _____ across the greasy road. (**skid**)

   b. The old man _____ for money for food to eat. (**beg**)

   c. The glass broke when he _____ it on the floor. (**drop**)

   d. The thieves _____ the hotel last night. (**rob**)

   e. Peter _____ his sister a woollen jumper. (**knit**)

   f. I _____ the sugar before I drank the tea. (**stir**)

   g. The class _____ to Melbourne by train. (**travel**)

   h. The leaking tap _____ all night. (**drip**)

2. Use the past tense verbs of the words in the box to complete the story. Hint! Some verbs change their spelling to make the past tense. You might need to say the verb aloud to see if it sounds right.

   ride   speak   tell   bring   ring   teach   get   eat   go   fly

Yesterday Tim _____ his bike to school. When he arrived he _____ to Lisa and _____ her he had _____ his kite to school. At nine o'clock he _____ the bell. In class the teacher _____ the children how to do long division. At recess Tim _____ a delicious cake from his lunch box and _____ it. Then he _____ out on to the oval where he _____ his kite.

35

© P. Clutterbuck, Good Grammar! Book 3. This page may be reproduced for classroom use.

Verb Tense

Name _____

The tense of a verb tells us when the action is, was, or will be carried out. Present tense refers to actions that are happening now, at this moment. Past tense refers to actions that happened in the past, a few seconds ago or years ago. Future tense refers to actions that will happen in the future, in a few seconds or in a few years.

Present tense: She *likes* the chocolate flavour.

Past tense: She *liked* the chocolate flavour.

Future tense: She *will like* the chocolate flavour.

1. Circle all the past tense verbs and underline all the present tense verbs. Then rewrite each joke in the future tense.

a. What do people do in a clock factory? They make faces all day.

_____

b. Why did the cross-eyed teacher quit? He couldn't control his pupils.

_____

c. What went over the tongue and through the eye? A shoelace.

_____

d. Why was the exterminator so sad? He couldn't bear to see the moth bawl.

_____

e. What did one eye say to the other eye? "Between you and me, something smells."

_____

f. Why was the chicken sick? It had people pox.

_____

2. Make up a joke of your own. Write it in the past tense and then in the future tense.

a. _____

b. _____

© P. Clutterbuck, Good Grammar! Book 3. This page may be reproduced for classroom use.

Verb Voice

Name _____ **Grammar BLM 20**

A verb can be in the active or the passive voice. The voice of the verb tells whether the subject is doing the action (active voice) or whether something is being done to the subject (passive voice). When the passive voice is used, the verb includes an auxiliary (helping verb) and a participle (main verb).

Active voice: **Katy *read* the book.**
Passive voice: **The book *was read* by Katy.**

1. Make these sentences more direct by rewriting them in the active voice.

a. A big, hairy spider was eaten by my dog.

_____

b. The games are chosen by the children.

_____

c. The flowers are picked by the gardener.

_____

d. Five goals were kicked by Ned.

_____

e. The car was crashed by my father.

_____

f. The children were snapped at by the injured dog.

_____

2. Make these public notices less aggressive by rewriting them in the passive voice.

a. Do not put your feet on the seats!

_____

b. Keep your dog on a lead!

_____

c. Put your rubbish in the bin!

_____

d. We do not allow running!

_____

© P. Clutterbuck, Good Grammar! Book 3. This page may be reproduced for classroom use.

Verbs

Verbs can be formed from other parts of speech.

1. Complete the sentence by making a verb from the noun in brackets.
a. The thief tried to _____ that she was innocent. (**proof**)
b. "I _____ we will arrive soon," said Tim. (**hopefulness**)
c. You will have to _____ well if you are going to come with us. (**behaviour**)
d. I did not _____ his incredible story. (**belief**)
e. The teacher asked me to _____ the chalkboard. (**cleanliness**)
f. We began to _____ loudly at his jokes. (**laughter**)

2. Write the verb for each of the following nouns.
a. departure _____
b. enjoyment _____
c. collection _____
d. preparation _____
e. pleasure _____
f. drawing _____
g. entrance _____
h. decoration _____
i. invitation _____
j. government _____

3. Write sentences using the following words as a. nouns and b. verbs.

dream	sail	point

a. noun: _____
b. verb: _____
a. noun: _____
b. verb: _____
a. noun: _____
b. verb: _____

© P. Clutterbuck, Good Grammar! Book 3. This page may be reproduced for classroom use.

Plural Verbs

Name _____ Grammar BLM **22**

If the subject of a sentence is plural the verb should be plural.
If the subject is singular the verb should be singular.
If there is more than one subject joined by *and* the verb should be plural.
Collective nouns usually take a singular verb.

1. Circle the subject. Then choose the correct word from the brackets.
   a. This dog _____ friendly. (is are)
   b. These dogs _____ friendly. (is are)
   c. We _____ going to the zoo. (am are)
   d. I _____ going to the zoo. (am are)
   e. She _____ faster than me. (runs run)
   f. They _____ faster than me. (runs run)

2. Circle the subject. Then choose the correct word from the brackets.
   a. A new pack of cards _____ opened. (was were)
   b. The swarm of bees _____ approaching. (is are)
   c. A school of whales _____ sighted off the coast. (was were)
   d. The party of climbers _____ returned from the mountain.
      (has have)
   e. The football team _____ tonight. (practises practise)
   f. A sack of potatoes _____ on the road. (is are)

3. Circle the subject. Then choose the correct word from the brackets.
   a. Mum and Dad _____ on their way. (is are)
   b. Here _____ the bride and groom.
      (comes come)
   c. Sarah and Zoe _____ going away today. (is are)
   d. The parents and teachers _____ every month. (meets meet)
   e. Jack and Freya _____ very hard. (works work)
   f. This is where Ned and Max _____ to meet me. (was were)

© P. Clutterbuck, Good Grammar! Book 3. This page may be reproduced for classroom use.

Adjectives

Introduction

Adjectives are words that tell us more about nouns or pronouns by describing them, adding detail or refining their meaning. By using adjectives, we can add meaning and interest to sentences. Children should also come to understand that a completely different picture can be produced by changing the adjectives in a sentence. Examples:

> The *resentful* girl showed the *cranky* lady the way.
> The *kind* girl showed the *old* lady the way.
> The *savage* dog chased the *frightened* boy.
> The *playful* dog chased the *laughing* boy.

Children should be encouraged to think about the adjectives they choose and to steer away from adjectives that have become meaningless through overuse, such as *nice* and *good*. Examples:

> A *nice* day.   A *sunny* day.
> A *good* story.   An *exciting* story.

When more than one adjective is used before a noun, the adjectives are arranged from the general to the specific. In the example 'the old, black, savage dogs' *old* is more general than *savage* so it is placed first.

An adjective can come before or after the noun or pronoun it is describing. Examples:

> *The big, black dog.*
> *The dog was big and black.*

There are many types of adjectives. Upper Primary children need to develop an awareness of the following types of adjectives and their uses.

(a) **Describing adjectives** are the most common. They are used to describe, or tell us about the quality of, a noun or pronoun. Examples:
> *new   old   beautiful   ugly   big   small*

(b) **Pointing adjectives** (sometimes called demonstrative adjectives or determiners) are used to point out which noun is being spoken of. Examples:
> *That* toy belongs to Katy.
> *This* toy belongs to me.
> *Those* boxes were taken away.
> *These* boxes were left behind.

(c) **Possessive adjectives** are used to show possession. Examples:
> This is *my* pen.

Here is *your* hat.
The possessive adjectives are:

	Singular	Plural
First person	my	our
Second person	your	your
Third person	his, her, its	their

(d) **Number adjectives** are used to show the number of things or the numerical order of things. Examples:

    cardinal: *two* horses   *ten* fingers

    ordinal: the *first* person in the queue   the *second* month

(e) **Indefinite adjectives** are also used to refer to number but they do not tell us the exact number. Examples:

    Some boys carried the tent.

    Much fuss was made over the new baby.

    Few suggestions were received.

    Many cars were held up in the traffic jam.

Adjectives can change their form to indicate **degrees of comparison**. The three degrees are:

- **Positive Degree** This is the normal form of the adjective. Examples:

    a sweet lolly   *a muddy boy*   *a beautiful rose*

- **Comparative Degree** This is used when we compare two people or things. We usually add *-er* to the adjective, but for longer words we sometimes put *more* in front of the adjective. Examples:

    a *sweeter* lolly   a *muddier* boy   a more *beautiful* rose

- **Superlative Degree** This is the highest degree and is used when we compare more than two people or things. It is made by adding *-est* to the adjective or putting *most* in front of the adjective. Examples:

    the *sweetest* lolly   the *muddiest* boy   the *most beautiful* rose

Things to remember:

- Some adjectives add *-er* or *-est* without any change to their spelling. Examples:

    tall   *taller*   *tallest*

- Adjectives that end in *-e* drop the *-e* when adding *-er* or *-est*. Examples:

    large   *larger*   *largest*

- If the adjective ends in *-y* the *-y* is changed to *-i* before adding *-er* or *-est*. Examples:

  heavy   heavier   heaviest

- In some adjectives the last letter is doubled before adding *-er* or *-est*. Examples:

  big   bigger   biggest

- Adjectives of three syllables (and even some of two syllables) have *more* before them for the comparative degree and *most* before them for the superlative degree. Examples:

  honest   more honest   most honest

- Some adjectives only have a positive degree. For example, a thing can only be *dead*, it cannot be more dead. Other examples:

  full   empty   straight   perfect   correct

To recognise an adjective, ask questions such as:

What kind of?

How many?

Which?

> *The old cars were demolished.*
> What kind of cars?   *old* (descriptive adjective)
> *Six flowers were in the glass vase.*
> How many flowers?   *six* (number adjective)
> What kind of vase?   *glass* (descriptive adjective)
> *Those girls are going fishing.*
> Which girls?   *those* (pointing adjective)

Teaching Strategies

Stretch the joke

Write a story, preferably a short joke, on the board. Underline all the nouns. Have children rewrite the story adding adjectives to the nouns.

Two caterpillars were eating grass in a garden when a butterfly flew overhead.

Two large, fat caterpillars were eating delicious grass . . .

Self-esteem adjectives

Have children describe each other using positive adjectives.

Tom is a happy boy.

Ellen is a fast runner.

Missing nouns

Give children a list of adjectives and have them add suitable nouns.

curly_____ delicious_____

black_____ sharp_____

three _____ savage _____

For sale

Have children add suitable adjectives to mock advertisements.

FOR SALE HOUSE, ROOF, ROOMS, GARAGE, ETC.

FOR SALE. LARGE HOUSE, TILE ROOF, EIGHT ROOMS, LOCK-UP GARAGE, ETC.

Opposites quiz

Read out a list of adjectives. Have children call out or write the opposites. This can be played in teams. The first team to score ten is the winning team.

stopping/starting   right/wrong   careless/careful

useful/useless   straight/bent

Portraits

Have children cut out a picture of a person (possibly someone well-known) from a magazine. Have them write sentences which include appropriate adjectives.

This lady has black hair.

She is leading two dogs.

Adjective mix-up

Divide the class into two groups. Ask one group to make a list of nouns. Ask the other group to make a list of adjectives. Now have the children try to fit each adjective beside a noun it could describe.

Adjective list	Noun list
empty	classroom
crowded	grass
long	bucket

Newspaper hunt

Have children read through newspapers and magazines and cut out any interesting adjectives they find. Make a large class adjective chart. Encourage children to refer to the chart when they need an adjective for their own writing.

Adjectives Formed From Nouns

Noun	Adjective	Noun	Adjective
accident	accidental	effect	effective
advantage	advantageous	energy	energetic
adventure	adventurous	expense	expensive
affection	affectionate	expression	expressive
ancestor	ancestral	fable	fabulous
angel	angelic	faith	faithful
anger	angry	fame	famous
anxiety	anxious	fashion	fashionable
athlete	athletic	fault	faulty
autumn	autumnal	favour	favourite
beauty	beautiful	fire	fiery
bible	biblical	fool	foolish
boy	boyish	fortune	fortunate
capacity	capacious	fraud	fraudulent
caution	cautious	friend	friendly
centre	central	fur	furry
charity	charitable	fury	furious
child	childish	giant	gigantic
choir	choral	girl	girlish
circle	circular	gold	golden
colony	colonial	grace	graceful
comfort	comfortable	grief	grievous
continent	continental	haste	hasty
courage	courageous	hero	heroic
coward	cowardly	humour	humorous
craft	crafty	hygiene	hygienic
credit	creditable	industry	industrial
crime	criminal	influence	influential
custom	customary	injury	injurious
danger	dangerous	labour	laborious
deceit	deceitful	luxury	luxurious
disaster	disastrous	man	manly
economy	economical	marvel	marvellous

© P. Clutterbuck, Good Grammar! Book 3. This page may be reproduced for classroom use.

Adjectives Formed From Nouns

Noun	Adjective	Noun	Adjective
melody	melodious	rebellion	rebellious
mercy	merciful	region	regional
metal	metallic	response	responsive
method	methodical	school	scholastic
miracle	miraculous	sense	sensible
mischief	mischievous	service	serviceable
misery	miserable	shower	showery
mountain	mountainous	skill	skilful
muscle	muscular	squalor	squalid
music	musical	star	starry
mystery	mysterious	sun	sunny
nation	national	suspicion	suspicious
nature	natural	sympathy	sympathetic
noise	noisy	tempest	tempestuous
nonsense	nonsensical	terror	terrible
occasion	occasional	triangle	triangular
ocean	oceanic	tribe	tribal
ornament	ornamental	value	valuable
peril	perilous	victory	victorious
person	personal	vigour	vigorous
picture	picturesque	water	watery
pirate	piratical	winter	wintry
poet	poetic	wool	woollen
poison	poisonous	wretch	wretched

© P. Clutterbuck, Good Grammar! Book 3. This page may be reproduced for classroom use.

ADJECTIVES

Describing Adjectives

amazing	dry	immense	scarlet
annoying	easy	khaki	scorched
auburn	elegant	large	secluded
beautiful	enormous	loud	violent
bright	exciting	marvellous	violet
dangerous	filthy	mauve	wrinkly
deserted	fresh	narrow	yellow
desolate	friendly	naughty	young
dirty	gorgeous	occasional	
disgusting	gruesome	polluted	
disobedient	hollow	rich	

Pointing Adjectives	Possessive Adjectives	Number Adjectives	Indefinite Adjectives
such	her	cardinal	all
that	his	hundred	any
these	its	two	few
this	my	ordinal	little
those	our	fifth	many
	their	second	much
	your		several
			some

© P. Clutterbuck, Good Grammar! Book 3. This page may be reproduced for classroom use.

Adjectives

Describing adjectives are used to describe a noun or pronoun.

1. Choose a word from the box to complete each sentence.

> circular   fragile   broad   careful   perilous   stupid

a. A river that is wide is_____.

b. Something easily broken is_____.

c. If something is round it is _____.

d. A foolish person is_____.

e. If something is dangerous it is _____.

f. If a person is cautious he or she is _____.

2. Choose the most suitable describing adjective from the box.

> delicious   rusty   sunny   savage   interesting   woollen   ripe   clever

a. _____ story

b. _____ student

c. _____ knife

d. _____ food

e. _____ jumper

f. _____ weather

g. _____ apple

h. _____ watchdog

3. Rewrite the story replacing each underlined adjective with one of a similar meaning from the box.

> big   minute   scared   thick   strong   high   sour   fat

As we walked through the <u>dense</u> forest we saw a <u>plump</u> bird eating some <u>bitter</u> fruit that grew on a <u>tall</u> tree. My brother Sam, a <u>sturdy</u> lad, threw a <u>tiny</u> pebble at the bird. The <u>frightened</u> bird flew to the safety of a <u>gigantic</u> bush.

_____

_____

_____

47

© P. Clutterbuck, Good Grammar! Book 3. This page may be reproduced for classroom use.

Adjectives

Name _____   Grammar BLM **24**

Describing adjectives are used to describe a noun or pronoun.

1. Choose the describing adjective from the box that has the opposite meaning to the adjective in the brackets.

> plump   foolish   dangerous   false   fresh   deep

a. This loaf of bread is _____. (**stale**)

b. This is a _____ spot to swim. (**safe**)

c. The pool is very _____ here. (**shallow**)

d. I knew his statement was _____. (**true**)

e. This pig is quite _____. (**thin**)

f. Tom is a _____ boy. (**wise**)

2. Choose the describing adjective from the box that has a similar meaning to the adjective in the brackets.

> careful   sudden   peculiar   serious   sharp   sacred

a. I found her to be a _____ person. (**odd**)

b. Paul is a very _____ boy. (**cautious**)

c. We were startled by the _____ movement. (**abrupt**)

d. It was a _____ breach of rules. (**grave**)

e. She felt a _____ pain in her arm. (**acute**)

f. We entered the _____ temple quietly. (**holy**)

3. If the adjectives have a similar meaning write S. If they have an opposite meaning write O.

a. plentiful   abundant   _____   e. cordial   friendly   _____

b. dreary   exciting   _____   f. feeble   strong   _____

c. soft   tender   _____   g. awkward   graceful   _____

d. private   public   _____   h. drowsy   sleepy   _____

48

© P. Clutterbuck, Good Grammar! Book 3. This page may be reproduced for classroom use.

Adjectives

Name _____ Grammar BLM **25**

Number adjectives are used to show the number of things or the
numerical order of things.
Indefinite adjectives are also used to refer to number but they do not
tell us the exact number.

1. Choose an adjective from the box to complete each sentence.

> twelve   three   two   ten   eight   four   fourteen   one hundred

a. There are _____ eggs in a dozen.

b. A bicycle has_____wheels.

c. There are_____years in a decade.

d. A tricycle has_____ wheels.

e. A century is_____years.

f. There are_____ days in a fortnight.

g. A square has _____sides.

h. An octopus has _____tentacles.

2. Choose the number adjective from the brackets to complete each sentence.

a. February is the_____ month. (**second hottest**)

b. I am the _____ person in the queue. (**first shortest**)

c. Did you see the_____ cyclist? (**hairy fourth**)

d. I would like the_____ book on that shelf please. (**fifth fat**)

e. Katy lives in the _____ house on Avenue Road. (**white third**)

f. The_____ swimmer stood on the blocks. (**cold sixth**)

3. Write sentences using the following as indefinite adjectives.

> some   few   many   most   much

a. _____

b. _____

c. _____

d. _____

e. _____

© P. Clutterbuck, Good Grammar! Book 3. This page may be reproduced for classroom use.

Adjectives

Name _____ **Grammar BLM**

Pointing adjectives are used to point out which noun is being spoken of.
That **toy belongs to Katy.**
This **toy belongs to me.**

1. Choose a pointing adjective from the box to complete each sentence.
    Then circle the noun that the adjective points out.

> those   these   this   such   that

a. _____ shoes are made of crocodile skin.

b. What are you going to do with_____ tables?

c. _____ cow had twin calves.

d. _____ day has been the worst day of my life.

e. _____ silliness is to be discouraged.

2. Now use the pointing adjectives in sentences of your own.
    In each sentence underline the adjective and circle the noun it points out.

a. _____

b. _____

c. _____

d. _____

e. _____

Possessive adjectives are used to show ownership.
This is *my* **pen.**
Here is *your* **hat.**

3. Underline the possessive adjectives.

a. My dog is very funny. He bites his tail as he runs around.

b. Your pencils are on the table next to our books.

c. Their cat is licking its paws.

d. Her bedroom is untidy but your bedroom is neat.

© P. Clutterbuck, Good Grammar! Book 3. This page may be reproduced for classroom use.

Adjectives

Adjectives can be formed from other parts of speech.

1. Complete each sentence by forming an adjective from the noun in brackets.

a. I fell asleep in the _____ chair. (**comfort**)

b. The _____ animal was captured by the park rangers. (**danger**)

c. It was a _____ day when the children left. (**storm**)

d. Mr Smith is a very _____ person. (**patience**)

e. This is an extremely _____ painting. (**value**)

f. The _____ film star visited our town recently. (**fame**)

2. Form an adjective from each noun.

a. anger   an _____ teacher   e. coward   a _____ act

b. child   a silly, _____ act   f. favour   my _____ food

c. friend   a _____ person   g. fur   a _____ rabbit

d. expense   an _____ perfume   h. haste   a _____ decision

3. Write sentences of your own using adjectives formed from the following nouns.

> noise   water   luxury   sense   mercy   nation

a. _____

b. _____

c. _____

d. _____

e. _____

f. _____

51

© P. Clutterbuck, Good Grammar! Book 3. This page may be reproduced for classroom use.

Adjectives

Proper adjectives are formed from proper nouns. Proper adjectives also begin with a capital letter.

1. Write the proper adjective formed from the proper noun in brackets.

   a. I ate some _____ food. (**China**)

   b. The guide showed us around the _____ village. (**Wales**)

   c. Is this a _____ watch? (**Switzerland**)

   d. The _____ flag is blue and white. (**Greece**)

   e. My mother's friend speaks with a _____ accent. (**Scotland**)

   f. My uncle bought a bottle of _____ wine. (**France**)

2. Write the proper adjective formed from the proper noun.

   a. Turkey _____   e. Mexico _____

   b. Sweden _____   f. Japan _____

   c. Britain _____   g. Italy _____

   d. Tibet _____   h. Egypt _____

3. The following athletes represent their countries. Underline the proper adjective and write the proper noun on the line.

   a. A Turkish runner won the marathon. _____

   b. A Dutch weight-lifter won the gold medal. _____

   c. An Irish athlete won the 200m hurdle. _____

   d. A Norwegian swimmer won her heat in the distance event. _____

   e. A Spanish team won the rowing event. _____

   f. A Brazilian boxer won the lightweight contest. _____

© P. Clutterbuck, Good Grammar! Book 3. This page may be reproduced for classroom use.

Adjectives

Adjectives can change their form to show degrees of comparison.

Positive Degree	Comparative Degree	Superlative Degree
sweet	sweeter	sweetest
muddy	muddier	muddiest
beautiful	more beautiful	most beautiful

1. Complete these sentences by writing the correct degree of the adjective in brackets.

a. This is the _____ building in the city. (**old**)

b. My puppy is _____ than your puppy. (**young**)

c. My brother is _____ than me. (**short**)

d. Today is _____ than yesterday. (**cold**)

e. Katy bought the _____ toy in the shop. (**dear**)

f. Tim's mouse was the _____ pet of all the pets at our show. (**small**)

2. Complete the table.

Positive degree	Comparative degree	Superlative degree
safe	safer	
wise		
pale		
		bravest
	larger	

3. Complete these sentences by writing the correct degree of the adjective in brackets. Hint! If the adjective has a short vowel and ends with a single consonant, the last letter is doubled before adding -er or -est.

a. These are the _____ apples in the supermarket. (**big**)

b. This pig is much _____ than that pig. (**fat**)

c. That story was the _____ I've ever heard. (**sad**)

d. Today was the _____ day we've had for ten years. (**hot**)

© P. Clutterbuck, Good Grammar! Book 3. This page may be reproduced for classroom use.

Adjectives

Name _____ Grammar BLM **30**

Adjectives can change their form to show degrees of comparison.

Positive Degree	Comparative Degree	Superlative Degree
sweet	sweeter	sweetest
muddy	muddier	muddiest
beautiful	more beautiful	most beautiful

1. Complete these sentences by writing the correct degree of the adjective in brackets. Hint! If the adjective ends in -y, change the -y to -i before adding -er or -est.

a. Mike must be the_____ boy in the whole school. (**busy**)

b. This box is much_____ than that one. (**heavy**)

c. You always seem to be_____ than I am. (**lucky**)

d. This kitten is the_____ of the whole litter. (**noisy**)

2. Circle the correct adjective. Hint! Some adjectives have irregular forms.

a. He is (**gooder better**) than me at marbles.

b. This is the (**worst baddest**) day I've had all year.

c. Joanne has (**littler less**) cherries than I have.

d. Tom is the (**morest most**) reliable boy in the grade.

3. Complete the chart. Hint! Adjectives of three syllables, and some of two syllables, have *more* written before them for the comparative degree and *most* for the superlative degree.

Positive Degree	Comparative Degree	Superlative Degree
beautiful		
	more honest	
efficient		
	more humorous	
		most delicious
sorrowful		
		most comfortable

© P. Clutterbuck, Good Grammar! Book 3. This page may be reproduced for classroom use.

Adverbs

Introduction

An **adverb** is a word that adds meaning to a verb, an adjective or another adverb.

There are many types of adverbs. The most important types for Upper Primary children to recognise are:

(a) **Adverbs of Place** These are used to show where something happens.
   I told him to come *here*. Other examples:
   > *above   behind   below   upstairs   outside   near   everywhere*

(b) **Adverbs of Time** These are used to show when something happens.
   He played *yesterday*. Other examples:
   > *soon   later   yesterday   today   often*
   > *seldom   never   already   now   then*

(c) **Adverbs of Manner** These are used to show how something happens.
   The child cried *loudly*. Other examples:
   > *quietly   furiously   helpfully   softly   gently   noisily*

(d) **Interrogative Adverbs** These ask questions.
   How are you? Other examples:
   > *when   whence   where   whither   why*

(e) **Negative or Modal Adverbs**   These make sentences negative, agree or express doubt.
   He is *not* coming. Other examples:
   > *never   no   not at all   perhaps   possibly   probably   yes*

Like adjectives, adverbs can change their form to indicate degrees of comparison. The three degrees are:
* **Positive Degree** This refers to one person or thing. Example:
   Tom can play *hard*.
* **Comparative Degree** This compares two people or things. Example:
   Tom can play *harder*.
* **Superlative Degree** This compares more than two people or things.
   Of the three children, Tom plays the *hardest*.

Things to remember:
* To adverbs of one syllable, add *-er* and *-est* to form the comparative and superlative. Examples:
   > *hard   harder   hardest*
* Adverbs that end in *-ly* have *more* and *most* placed before them to form the comparative and superlative. Examples:
   > *silently   more silently   most silently*

- Some adverbs are irregular, and must be learnt individually. Examples:

badly	*worse*	*worst*
well	*better*	*best*
much	*more*	*most*

- Some adverbs look like adjectives. You can tell they are adverbs if they add meaning to verbs, adjectives and other adverbs. If they add meaning to a noun, they are adjectives.

Teaching Strategies

Give me one

Have children provide one word to replace a group of words in a sentence that is written on the chalkboard.
Mike always drives in a fast way.
Mike always drives quickly.

How, when or where?

Have children add words to a sentence written on the chalkboard. The words should tell how, when, or where the action happened.
Mike's bike was stolen . . . (when)   yesterday
The teacher told me to put it over . . . (where)   there
Billy did her work . . . (how)   neatly

Adverb list

Have children list suitable adverbs to complete a sentence.
I can walk . . .
quickly   slowly   rapidly   proudly   lazily   awkwardly
Other suitable verbs to use for this exercise include: swim, speak, creep, sleep, fights, wait, eat, laugh, dance, read, etc.

Similar or opposite?

Call out an adverb or write an adverb on the chalkboard. Have children provide an adverb of similar meaning or one of opposite meaning.
rapidly: quickly   slowly
loudly: noisily   softly

Act the adverb

Have children carry out a number of actions in different manners.
Walk: quickly   carefully   foolishly

WORD BANK

ADVERBS

Adverbs of Place

above
behind
below
downstairs
elsewhere
everywhere
here
inside
near
nowhere
outside
somewhere
upstairs
within
yonder

Adverbs of Time

already
immediately
instantly
late
lately
meanwhile
never
now
often
presently
recently
seldom
shortly
soon
then
today
yesterday
yet

Adverbs of Manner

anxiously
carefully
desperately
furiously
helpfully
ill
jauntily
loudly
nervously
noisily
powerfully
quietly
rapidly
skilfully
so
tearfully
trustingly
urgently
vigorously
well

Interrogative Adverbs

how
when
whence
where
whither
why

Negative or Modal Adverbs

never
no
not
not at all
perhaps
possibly
probably

57

© P. Clutterbuck, Good Grammar! Book 3. This page may be reproduced for classroom use.

Adverbs

An adverb is a word that adds meaning to a verb, an adjective or another adverb.

1. Select the best adverb to complete each sentence.

> gracefully   neatly   busily   angrily
> brightly   tightly   softly   carefully

   a. We should cross a busy street _____ .
   b. We tie parcels_____ .
   c. Lights can shine _____.
   d. We should write_____ in our books.
   e. The children worked_____.
   f. The lion roared _____ .
   g. We should whisper_____ .
   h. A swan swims_____ .

2. Beside each adverb write *how, when* or *where* to show what it tells us.

   a. tomorrow _____   f. yesterday_____
   b. greedily_____   g. inside _____
   c. tonight_____   h. down _____
   d. today_____   i. sweetly_____
   e. sadly_____   j. outside _____

3. Add an adverb of your own to complete each sentence.
    Make sure your adverb answers the word in brackets.

   a. She fell _____ . (where)
   b. He whistled_____ . (how)
   c. Tom arrived _____. (when)
   d. The window was broken_____ . (how)
   e. The kangaroo jumped the fence _____. (how)
   f. I will repay you_____ . (when)

© P. Clutterbuck, Good Grammar! Book 3. This page may be reproduced for classroom use.

Adverbs

Name _____   **Grammar BLM** `32`

An adverb is a word that adds meaning to a verb, an adjective or another adverb.

1. Select the best adverb telling *where* to complete each sentence.

> out   everywhere   there   here   inside
> nowhere   below   somewhere

a. Put the boxes over_____ .

b. The lost pens were_____ to be found.

c. I can't find it but I must have put it_____ .

d. Let's sit right _____ .

e. They stayed on the top deck but I went_____ .

f. When she dropped the bottle the water spilled _____ .

g. He was so angry he stormed_____ .

h. Tim went outside but I stayed _____ .

2. Add an adverb telling *how* to each verb.

> politely   swiftly   softl   loudly
> heavily   happily   slowly   sweetly

a. fell_____   e. yelled _____

b. whispered_____   f. limped_____

c. sang_____   g. spoke_____

d. ran _____   h. played_____

3. To each pair of sentences add an adverb telling *where* and then an adverb telling *how*.

a. Ben played _____ .   Ben played _____.

b. I told her to come _____.   I told her to come_____.

c. The fish swam _____ .   The fish swam_____.

59

© P. Clutterbuck, Good Grammar! Book 3. This page may be reproduced for classroom use.

Adverbs

An adverb is a word that adds meaning to a verb, an adjective or another adverb.

1. Write an adverb to replace the words in brackets.
   a. The old man was sleeping (**in peace**). _____
   b. Our teacher left the room (**in a hurry**). _____
   c. Lisa jumped the fence (**with ease**). _____
   d. We are going to leave (**in a short time**). _____
   e. Tim arrived (**after the expected time**). _____
   f. He gazed (**with pride**) at his good writing. _____

2. Add an adverb from the box to complete each sentence.

   | wearily | here | upstairs | now | noisily |
   | tomorrow | tonight | punctually |

   a. We must leave right_____ .
   b. Put it_____ .
   c. Paul arrived _____.
   d. Ben yawned_____ .
   e. The stars are shining brightly _____.
   f. The match will be played_____ .
   g. There was a party_____ .
   h. The monkeys chattered _____.

3. Add an adverb of your own to complete each sentence.
   a. The children wandered _____.
   b. Sally always speaks_____ .
   c. I cuddled the baby rabbit_____ .
   d. Mike crossed the busy road_____ .
   e. The man fell_____ .

© P. Clutterbuck, Good Grammar! Book 3. This page may be reproduced for classroom use.

Adverbs

An adverb is a word that adds meaning to a verb, an adjective or another adverb.

1. Write the adverb that has a similar meaning.

tidily	feebly	glumly	foolishly
abruptly	gently	gladly	rapidly

a. weakly_____
b. happily_____
c. neatly_____
d. stupidly_____

e. softly_____
f. sadly_____
g. suddenly_____
h. quickly_____

2. Write the adverb that has the opposite meaning.

swiftly	angrily	politely	neatly
bravely	suddenly	later	yesterday

a. untidily_____
b. slowly_____
c. happily_____
d. cowardly_____

e. rudely_____
f. tomorrow_____
g. gradually_____
h. immediately_____

3. If the adverbs have a similar meaning write S. If they have the opposite meaning write O.

a. always   never_____
b. angrily   wildly_____
c. there   here _____
d. sometimes   always_____
e. lazily   idly_____
f. carefully   carelessly_____
g. gracefully   awkwardly_____
h. distinctly   clearly_____

61

© P. Clutterbuck, Good Grammar! Book 3. This page may be reproduced for classroom use.

Adverbs

Adverbs can be formed from other parts of speech.

1. Complete each sentence by forming an adverb from the adjective in brackets.

   a. The girl sang _____ . (sweet)

   b. We waited _____ . (patient)

   c. Sam ran _____ . (quick)

   d. The crash happened _____ . (sudden)

   e. She accepted the food _____ . (glad)

   f. Sam is feeling _____ . (poor)

2. Complete each sentence by forming an adverb from the adjective in brackets. Hint!
   If the adjective ends in -y, change the -y to -i before adding -ly.

   a. We did the work _____ . (easy)

   b. The dog ate the food _____ . (greedy)

   c. He is dressed _____ . (shabby)

   d. She fell _____ . (clumsy)

   e. He walked _____ around the house. (lazy)

   f. They sang the song _____ . (merry)

3. Complete each sentence by forming an adverb from an adjective in the box. Hint!
   If the adjective ends in -e, drop the -e before adding -ly to make the adverb.

   | humble   idle   feeble   gentle   comfortable |

   a. He nursed the baby _____ .

   b. She sat _____ in the chair.

   c. He accepted the prize _____ .

   d. The boy lazed _____ .

   e. The ill man walked _____ .

© P. Clutterbuck, Good Grammar! Book 3. This page may be reproduced for classroom use.

Articles

Introduction

There are three articles: *the*, *a* and *an*. Articles can be either **definite** or **indefinite**. Upper Primary children should be able to identify definite and indefinite articles.

(a) *The* is the **definite** article. It is definite because it is referring to a specific thing. Examples:

> *The* man who lives next door.   *The* dog is outside.

(b) *A* and *an* are **indefinite**. Rather than referring to a specific thing, they refer to any one of a group of things. Examples:

> *A* man lives next door.   *A* dog is outside.

An is used instead of *a* in front of words that begin with a vowel (a, e, i, o, u). *An* is also used in front of words that begin with a silent *h*. Examples:

> *an* apple   *an* egg   *an* igloo   *an* orange   *an* umbrella   *an* hour
> but   *a* hotel

Teaching Strategies

The missing article

Allow children to develop their own paragraphs or short stories leaving out the articles *the*, *a* and *an*. They can then give the puzzles to their classmates to solve.

Make it definite

Have children change an indefinite article to the definite article, adding descriptive words to help.

> *I saw a dog.*
> *I saw the big, black dog.*

A or an?

Provide lists of words. Have children add *a* or *an* to introduce each.

> _____ *box* ____ *egg*

Articles

Name _____ **Grammar BLM**

Use *an* instead of *a* in front of words that begin with a vowel.

1. Write *a* or *an* in the spaces.

a. One day _____ man saw _____ monkey climbing _____ tall tree in _____ dense jungle.

b. Mike ate _____ orange and _____ apple for his lunch. Sometime later he ate _____ pie.

c. _____ athlete must train hard if she is to win _____ race.

d. On our farm there are lots of hens. One hen laid _____ egg on _____ branch of _____ tall tree.

e. Sue has _____ aunt who lives in Broadmeadows and _____ uncle who lives in Brisbane.

2. Write *a* or *an* in the spaces.

a. _____ orange

b. _____ underarm bowl

c. _____ dozen eggs

d. _____ big shed

e. _____ ocean liner

f. _____ book

g. _____ endangered species

h. _____ effective cure

i. _____ paper envelope

j. _____ obvious mistake

© P. Clutterbuck, Good Grammar! Book 3. This page may be reproduced for classroom use.

Articles

When we are talking about a particular thing, we use *the*. This is called the definite article.

When we are talking about a general thing, we use *a* or *an*. This is called the indefinite article.

Add *the, an*, or *a* in the spaces.

a. One day _____ old man was walking along _____ street. _____ man was wearing _____ orange shirt and _____ tie he was wearing had black and gold stripes. _____ lady who saw him in _____ supermarket was amused. _____ lady began to laugh at him. _____ old man said she was _____ rude person and he told her that he was going to _____ fancy dress ball.

b. Would you like to see _____ new car in the garage? It is _____ only car in this area that has _____ oil cleaning device that _____ engine cleans at all times. _____ uncle of mine had _____ car like it and he said it was _____ excellent device and _____ asset to all new cars.

c. Would you like _____ pink guinea pig? I have one. It is _____ only pink guinea pig in _____ world. I brought it from _____ old lady I met at _____ pet shop. She said she also had _____ blue rabbit and ostrich that had red and white stripes. She said _____ ostrich was _____ obstinate bird and laid _____ egg every day.

© P. Clutterbuck, Good Grammar! Book 3. This page may be reproduced for classroom use.

Articles

Name _____ Grammar BLM **38**

When we are talking about a particular thing, we use *the*. This is called the definite article.
When we are talking about a general thing, we use *a* or *an*. This is called the indefinite article.

1. Complete these sentences in your own words. You must include the article in brackets.

a. (the)   A horse galloped _____ .

b. (an)   I picked _____ .

c. (a)   I saw _____ .

d. (the)   Did you see _____ ?

e. (an)   In the jungle I saw _____ .

f. (a)   The boys found _____ .

2. Write *a* or *an* in the spaces.

a. There is _____ apple tree, _____ orange tree, _____ banana tree

   and _____ lemon tree in our garden.

b. I picked _____ onion, _____ lettuce, _____ radish and _____

   eggplant from our garden.

c. On the merry-go-round there is _____ zebra, _____ elephant, _____

   ape and _____ giraffe.

d. Some birds we saw were _____ ostrich, _____ emu, _____ robin,

   and _____ eagle.

e. There is _____ oak tree, _____ elm tree, _____ maple tree and

   _____ ash tree growing in the forest.

f. In the game the children had to point to _____ ear, _____ foot, _____

   ankle and _____ nose.

© P. Clutterbuck, Good Grammar! Book 3. This page may be reproduced for classroom use.

Articles

When we are talking about a particular thing, we use *the*. This is called the definite article.

When we are talking about a general thing, we use *a* or *an*. This is called the indefinite article.

1. Add *a* or *an* in the spaces

a. _____ novel excuse

b. _____ octagon

c. _____ mysterious event

d. _____ official complaint

e. in _____ instant

f. _____ incompetent person

g. _____ nugget of gold

h. _____ offensive smell

i. _____ audible sound

j. _____ angry cat

2. Add *a*, *an* or *the* in the spaces.

a. _____ company hired _____ assistant to help at _____ auction that was being held at _____ saleyards in _____ small country town. _____ assistant did not like _____ attitude of _____ manager of _____ company so he left immediately. Everyone thought this was _____ awful thing to do as it was very close to _____ day of _____ sale.

b. My mother is _____ expert cook. She cooked _____ enormous cake last year and won _____ prize at _____ show. After she had added _____ flour to _____ bowl she cracked _____ egg. She dropped _____ egg into _____ bowl and mixed it in. She put _____ cake in _____ oven to cook for forty minutes. When it had cooled she put it on _____ plate and cut it with _____ sharp knife.

© P. Clutterbuck, Good Grammar! Book 3. This page may be reproduced for classroom use.

Prepositions

Introduction

Prepositions are words we use to show the relationship of a noun or a pronoun to another word in the sentence. They can be called **place words** because they often tell us the position of things.

The puppy *is on* the chair.
The girl is *beside* the chair.
The bone is *under* the chair.

The prepositions *on, beside* and *under* all refer to the noun *chair*. They tell us the relationship between it and the puppy, the girl and the bone.

Problem prepositions

among/between

Something is shared among several people (three or more). Something is shared between two people. Examples:

> *I shared the cake among the whole grade.*
> *I shared the cake between Mary and myself.*

in/into

In shows position in one place. *Into* shows movement from one place to another. Examples:

> *The teacher is in the room.*
> *The boy dived into the river.*

different from

One thing or person is different from another. Never say *different than*.

beside/besides

Beside means at the side of. *Besides* means in addition to. Examples:

> *The teacher stood beside the table.*
> *Several girls were there besides Margaret.*

Preposition or adverb?

Some prepositions may look like adverbs. To tell whether the word is a preposition or an adverb, look at the way it is used. Look at the following sentences.

I fell down.   *Down* is an adverb of place. It tells where I fell.

I walked down the road. *Down* is a preposition governing road.

Remember also that a preposition usually has a noun or pronoun after it.

Teaching Strategies

Question time

Ask children to describe the position of some objects in the classroom. Tell children they must reply using a preposition in a sentence.

> *Where is the clock?*   *The clock is under the picture.*
> *Where is the television?*   *The television is beside the table.*

Preposition opposites

Have children provide the opposites of given prepositions.

> *The snake crawled over the rock.*
> *The snake crawled under the rock.*

Jumbled prepositions

Give children exercises in which the prepositions are jumbled. Have children identify the preposition or write it correctly.

> *The bird flew (voer) the tree.*
> *The bird flew over the tree.*

Preposition search

Photocopy a passage from a book with which the children are familiar. Have them work in groups to find the prepositions. Groups can then report back to the rest of the class.

WORD BANK

PREPOSITIONS

aboard	beyond	opposite
about	by	out of
above	despite	outside
across	down	over
after	during	past
against	except	round
along	for	since
among	from	through
around	in	to
at	in front of	towards
away	inside	under
because of	into	underneath
before	near	until
behind	next to	up
below	of	upon
beneath	off	with
beside	on	within
between	onto	without

© P. Clutterbuck, Good Grammar! Book 3. This page may be reproduced for classroom use.

Prepositions

Name _____ Grammar BLM **40**

Prepositions show the relationship of a noun or a pronoun to another word in the sentence. They are usually followed by a noun or a pronoun.

1. Complete each sentence by adding a preposition from the box.

> at   between   from   with   under   down

a. A line of cars stretched _____ the crossroads to the shopping centre.

b. The lollies were shared _____ Mary and Sally.

c. The dog growled _____ the two strangers.

d. I told her not to interfere _____ the new bicycle.

e. The snake slithered _____ the rock.

f. Jack and Jill tripped and rolled _____ the hill.

2. Unjumble the preposition.

a. Mike is standing _____ Pete. (**ebsdei**)

b. The cat is _____ the tree. (**enar**)

c. It is leaning _____ the fence. (**gaainst**)

d. They ran _____ the garden. (**raound**)

e. The ball is _____ the table. (**duner**)

f. The children ran _____ the playground. (**rthough**)

3. Write the missing preposition.

a. I disagree _____ him.

b. This is similar _____ that.

c. I have to rely _____ you.

d. He was found guilty _____ treason.

e. She was satisfied _____ the agreement.

71

© P. Clutterbuck, Good Grammar! Book 3. This page may be reproduced for classroom use.

Prepositions

Prepositions show the relationship of a noun or a pronoun to another word in the sentence. They are usually followed by a noun or a pronoun.

1. Circle the correct preposition in the brackets.

a. The key was found still (into   beside   in) the lock.

b. The box of books was (off   towards   on) the table.

c. The frightened horse galloped (across   since   among) the paddock.

d. She slipped and fell (up   down   through) the well.

e. Mike leant the shovel (below   from   against) the wall.

f. I picked the apples (of   during   off) the tree.

2. Add different prepositions to give each sentence in the pair a different meaning.

a. The vase was_____ the table.

   The vase was _____ the table.

b. The children ran _____ the tree.

   The children ran _____ the tree.

c. The jet landed_____ the airport.

   The jet landed_____ the airport.

3. Write sentences of your own using the prepositions in the box.

> against   over   under   between   off   below   near   down

a. _____

b. _____

c. _____

d. _____

e. _____

f. _____

© P. Clutterbuck, Good Grammar! Book 3. This page may be reproduced for classroom use.

Prepositions

Prepositions show the relationship of a noun or a pronoun to another word in the sentence. They are usually followed by a noun or a pronoun.

1. In each sentence circle the preposition and underline the two words that it relates.

a. We played on the oval.

b. We went to the farm.

c. I looked underneath the table.

d. I sat on the lawn.

e. Tom went through the trees.

2. Circle the prepositions in the grid and then use them to fill the spaces in the sentences.

t	h	r	o	u	g	h
o	f	p	d	w	o	i
v	r	a	o	i	f	n
e	o	s	w	t	f	t
r	m	t	n	h	x	o

a. Your bike is different_____ mine.

b. He dived from the board _____ the water.

c. I walked _____ my old school again.

d. I walked _____ the thick grass.

e. The lamp was knocked _____ the table.

f. The kangaroo jumped _____ the fence.

g. Mike slipped and fell _____ the hole.

h. Do not interfere _____ the new bikes.

© P. Clutterbuck, Good Grammar! Book 3. This page may be reproduced for classroom use.

Pronouns

Introduction

Upper Primary children should understand that we use **pronouns** to take the place of **nouns**. By using pronouns we can talk about people or things without naming them. This helps to stop our language becoming disjointed because of too much repetition.

Without pronouns we would have to write:

> *Bill said that Bill could not come because Bill's father had not brought Bill a new pair of sneakers.*

Children can quickly see the need for pronouns when they read this.

There are many types of pronouns. Those appropriate for Upper Primary children are:

(a) **Personal pronouns** Here are the personal pronouns that Upper Primary children should be familiar with and be able to use without difficulty.

	Nominative		Objective	
	Singular	**Plural**	**Singular**	**Plural**
First person	I	we	me	us
Second person	you	you	you	you
Third person	he, she, it	they	him, her, it	them

Things to remember:

- If a pronoun is the **subject** or part of the subject of a sentence, it is in the **nominative** case. Example:

    She is coming to my house.

    If a pronoun is the **object** or indirect object of a sentence, it is in the **objective** case. Example:

    I will play with *her*.

- **First person** pronouns are used if we are talking about ourselves. Examples:

    I am nine years old.

    We are learning about sharks.

    Second person pronouns are used if we are talking to someone. Example:

    Are *you* going to be long?

Third person pronouns are used if we are talking about someone or something else. Examples:

> *She* was late for school.
> *They* arrived by bus.
> *It* was on the table.

(b) **Possessive pronouns** Upper Primary children should also be familiar with the following possessive pronouns.

	Singular	Plural
First person	mine	ours
Second person	yours	yours
Third person	his, hers, its	theirs

Remember, some words look like pronouns but are really possessive adjectives. Look at the following sentences.

That book is *his*. *His* is a possessive pronoun showing ownership.
His book is on the table. *His* is a possessive adjective describing *book*.
For more information about possessive adjectives, see the chapter on adjectives.

(c) **Relative pronouns** These not only take the place of nouns but also help join sentences. The main relative pronouns are:

> *who*   *whom*   *which*   *that*

Who and **whom** are used to refer to people. *Who* is nominative case and is used when referring to the subject of the verb. *Whom* is objective case and is used when referring to the object of the verb. Examples:

> The girl *who* wore the blue hat.
> The friend with *whom* I went to the park.

Which and **that** are used to refer to animals, places and things.

(d) **Interrogative pronouns** These pronouns ask questions. Examples:

> *Who* paid?
> *What* is that?

Other interrogative pronouns are:

> *whom*   *whose*   *which*

However if the word is followed by a noun it is not an interrogative pronoun. It is an interrogative adjective.

(e) **Demonstrative pronouns** These are pronouns that stand for and point out nouns. Example:

> *This* is the train for Sydney.

Other demonstrative pronouns are:

> *that*   *those*   *these*

However if the word is followed by a noun it is not a demonstrative pronoun. It is a demonstrative adjective.

(f) **Indefinite pronouns** These pronouns stand for a person, place or thing which is not particularly defined. They usually take a singular verb. Example:

Is *anyone* interested in football?

Other indefinite pronouns are:

one	*none*	*somebody*	*everyone*	*someone*
everything	*anybody*	*anything*	*no-one*	*nobody*

Problem pronouns
its/it's
Its is a pronoun that means belonging to it. *It's* is not a pronoun. It is an abbreviation of *it is*.

I/me
Sometimes it is difficult to decide when to use *I* or *me* in a sentence. If in doubt, divide the sentence into two short sentences.

Mike is going to the circus.
I am going to the circus.
So the correct usage is: *Mike and I are going to the circus.*
Jack told Sally to get off the grass.
Jack told me to get off the grass.
So the correct usage is: *Jack told Sally and me to get off the grass.*

Teaching Strategies
Pronoun cloze
Write a passage on the chalkboard, leaving spaces for the pronouns. Write the missing pronouns on small pieces of cardboard and have children work in groups to stick them in the correct spaces using Blu-Tack.
Jane carried the glass to the kitchen. At the sink _____ dropped _____.

Pronoun search
Conduct a pronoun search from a common text, such as a photocopy of a story or poem already read. Have children read the text and circle any pronouns they find.

Buzz!
Read a short passage aloud. Tell children that when they hear a pronoun they must shout out 'Buzz!'. (You might first want to practise with one sentence.) Points can be awarded for correctly identifying the pronouns.

Pronouns

Name _____   **Grammar BLM** **43**

Pronouns are words that take the place of nouns.

1. Rewrite each sentence replacing the underlined words with a pronoun.

a. The lady said that <u>the lady</u> was leaving now.

_____

b. When the dog stopped barking it went back to <u>the dog's</u> kennel.

_____

c. The teacher told them that <u>the teacher</u> wanted them to work harder.

_____

d. The puppies whimpered when <u>the puppies</u> were hungry.

_____

e. The queen dismissed <u>the queen's</u> servants.

_____

f. Tom's father asked <u>Tom</u> to cut the wood.

_____

2. Colour the boxes that contain a pronoun.

we	paper	us	he
their	they	you	window
rabbit	jealous	my	mine
them	quickly	she	shiny
table	yours	over	silver

77

© P. Clutterbuck, Good Grammar! Book 3. This page may be reproduced for classroom use.

Pronouns

Name _____ Grammar BLM **44**

Pronouns are words that take the place of nouns.

1. Add a possessive pronoun to complete each sentence.

> yours   theirs   hers   his   mine   ours   its

a. This dog belongs to him. This dog is _____ .
b. This book belongs to Sally. This book is _____ .
c. This cup belongs to me. This cup is _____ .
d. We must take responsibility. The responsibility is _____ .
e. The horses belong to them. The horses are _____ .
f. This pen belongs to you. This pen is _____ .
g. This collar belongs to the dog. This collar is _____ .

2. Use the pronouns in the box to complete the story.

> he   she   her   they   it   him   mine   their

Last Tuesday the boys decided_____would go fishing. They put all_____ gear in the boot of the car. Mary was angry because the boys had put _____ rod in the car. It made her feel upset because _____ had only got the rod last week. She told her father and _____ agreed with her and asked the boys to put _____ back in the shed. Sam protested. "It is _____ !" he said. Mary began to cry. "I will not let _____ have it!" she said.

3. Circle the noun that the underlined pronoun refers to.

a. Lisa called the puppy to the kitchen so <u>she</u> could wash it.
b. Jack and Jill went up the hill but <u>he</u> slipped and fell down.
c. My father bought some lollies. He gave <u>them</u> to me.
d. These flowers are from my little sister. <u>She</u> picked them for you.

78

© P. Clutterbuck, Good Grammar! Book 3. This page may be reproduced for classroom use.

Pronouns

Name _____   **Grammar BLM** 45

Pronouns are words that take the place of nouns.

1. Use a possessive pronoun from the box to complete each sentence.

> their   his   our   my   ours   its   mine   her

a. I rode _____ bike to the cricket match.

b. Sally looked after _____ dogs while we were away.

c. I can't see Billy. Is that _____ bike there?

d. Mr and Mrs Smith have arrived. _____ car is in the driveway.

e. Sally left _____ case in the classroom.

f. Don't touch these pencils. They are _____ .

g. The dog hurt _____ leg when it was run over.

h. They grow carrots too but _____ are much better.

2. Circle the correct word in the brackets.

a. (My Me) friend said he would fight (you your) later.

b. That house is (our ours). Which house is (your yours)?

c. Sally said this is (hers her). Does she know it is really (their theirs)?

d. The stolen car is in (their theirs) garage. I think the car is (ours our).

e. That is (our ours) dog. Where is (yours your)?

3. Find the pronouns in the grid. Write each in a sentence.

m	i	n	e	h
o	u	r	s	e
y	o	u	r	r
t	h	e	i	r

a. _____

b. _____

c. _____

d. _____

e. _____

79

© P. Clutterbuck, Good Grammar! Book 3. This page may be reproduced for classroom use.

Pronouns

Demonstrative pronouns take the place of and point out a noun. However if the word is followed by a noun it is not a demonstrative pronoun. It is a demonstrative adjective.

This **is the train for Sydney.**   demonstrative pronoun
This **train is the train for Sydney.** demonstrative adjective

1. Circle the demonstrative pronouns. Underline the demonstrative adjectives.

a. Those teachers are leaving.

b. This is easy.

c. These are very expensive.

d. That is enough.

e. These need to be cared for.

f. That bus is going to Sydney.

g. These were given to me by Sam.

h. That is an awful picture.

2. Write sentences of your own using these words as demonstrative pronouns.

> that   this   those   these

a. _____

b. _____

c. _____

d. _____

3. Now write sentences using the same words as demonstrative adjectives.

a. _____

b. _____

c. _____

d. _____

© P. Clutterbuck, Good Grammar! Book 3. This page may be reproduced for classroom use.

Pronouns

Interrogative pronouns are used to ask questions. However if the word is followed by a noun it is not an interrogative pronoun. It is an interrogative adjective.

What **is the time?**   **interrogative pronoun**

What **train is that?**   **interrogative adjective**

1. Circle the interrogative pronouns. Underline the interrogative adjectives.

a. What is going to happen next?

b. Whose is it?

c. What answer did you give?

d. Which is the largest?

e. Which bus will you catch?

f. Who is that?

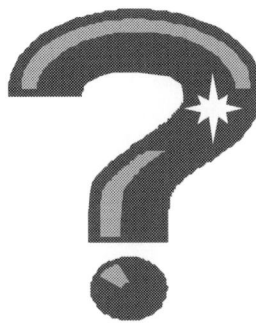

2. Write sentences of your own using these words as interrogative pronouns.

> who   whose   which   what

a. _____

b. _____

c. _____

d. _____

3. Now write sentences using the same words as interrogative adjectives.

a. _____

b. _____

c. _____

d. _____

81

© P. Clutterbuck, Good Grammar! Book 3. This page may be reproduced for classroom use.

Conjunctions

Introduction

Conjunctions are words that are used to join words or groups of words. Examples:

> Peter *and* John rode their bikes.
> We did not come. We were ill. We did not come *because* we were ill.

There are different types of conjunctions. Upper Primary children should be able to recognise and use the following:

(a) **Co-ordinating conjunctions** These join parts of a sentence that are of a similar type and of equal importance. Examples:

> I like fish *and* chips. (nouns linked)
> The dog ran across the yard *and* into its kennel. (two adverbial phrases linked)
> My team played well *but* it was beaten (two main clauses joined)

The most common co-ordinating conjunctions are:

> *and   but   for   nor   or   so   yet*

(b) **Subordinating conjunctions** These are used to join a subordinate clause (adverb clause, adjective clause, noun clause) to the rest of the sentence. Example:

> We lost the match *because* we played badly.

Some common subordinating conjunctions are:

> | *after* | *although* | *as* | *because* | *before* |
> | *once* | *since* | *than* | *though* | *unless* |
> | *until* | *when* | *whenever* | *where* | *wherever* | *while* |

(c) **Correlative conjunctions** These are conjunctions that are used in pairs. Examples:

> You can have *either* eggs *or* bacon for breakfast.
> She is *neither* tall *nor* short.
> Her brother is *both* handsome *and* intelligent.
> *Whether* it grows *or* not matters little.
> Other correlative conjunctions are:
> *as . . . as   not only . . . but also   not . . . but*

Conjunctions usually occur between the things they are joining, but this is not always so. A sentence can begin with a conjunction thus:

> *While in Sydney I visited the Opera House.*

In the past it was frowned upon to begin a sentence with *and* or *but*. Today it is acceptable to do so when you have good reason, such as for particular effect. Example:

> *He found his keys. He found his car. He found his wallet. And he found happiness again.*

Teaching Strategies

Conjunction search
Conduct a conjunction search from a common text, such as a photocopy of a story or poem already read. Have children read the text and circle any conjunctions they find.

Which conjunction?
Have children orally suggest suitable conjunctions for sentences which you read out loud.
I cannot come. My leg is sore.(if, because . . .)

In the beginning
Remind students that a conjunction need not necessarily come in the middle to join two sentences. Provide exercises encouraging children to begin the sentence with the conjunction.
He did not come. He is ill.
He did not come because he is ill.
Because he is ill, he did not come.

What's your excuse?
Have children make up reasonable or crazy excuses for certain things.
I could not do my homework because Mum locked me in a cupboard.
I had to play test cricket for Australia.
I went to the moon.

Edit and
To emphasise that some children overuse the conjunction *and*, write a passage on the chalkboard and have children suggest how it could be rewritten in a more interesting way.
I raced away quickly and out of the corner of my eye I saw a dog chasing me and it was barking loudly and I ran across the lawn and the dog followed after me and it was frothing at the mouth.

Brainstorm
Have children brainstorm pairs of phrases using *but* to join the two different ideas.
slow but steady   small but strong
They could also brainstorm pairs of words often associated with each other and joined with *and*.
Jack and Jill   bread and butter
steak and eggs   salt and pepper

WORD BANK   CONJUNCTIONS

Subordinating Conjunctions

after	though
although	unless
as	when
because	whenever
before	where
since	wherever
so long as	whether
than	while
that	

Correlative Conjunctions

as . . .as
both . . . and
either . . . or
neither . . . nor
not . . . but
not only . . . but also
whether . . . or

Co-ordinating Conjunctions

and
but
for
or
whereas

© P. Clutterbuck, Good Grammar! Book 3. This page may be reproduced for classroom use.

Conjunctions

Name _____ Grammar BLM **48**

Conjunctions are joining words. They are used to join words and groups of words.

1. Use the conjunctions in the box to complete the story.

(yet   when   since   because   unless   and   although)

John thought about not going _____ it was so cold. He had not seen Bill
_____ last December _____ they had met in the city one day. That
day John _____ Bill had renewed their friendship. _____ John
was older than Bill the two boys still had a lot in common. John had been
born two years before Bill _____ they were both born on May 12.
John decided he would go to see Bill _____ it started to snow.

2. Use the conjunction <u>and</u> to pair each word in box A to a word in Box B.

Box A (salt   knife   bread
up   round   thick
fish   oranges)

Box B (chips   down
lemons   butter   thin
round   pepper   fork)

a. _____   e. _____
b. _____   f. _____
c. _____   g. _____
d. _____   h. _____

3. Use a suitable conjunction to complete each sentence.
a. I wanted to go to the football _____ I didn't have any money.
b. My parents were angry _____ I was two hours late.
c. He said I could have it _____ I gave him ten dollars.
d. Sally swept the floor _____ I did the washing up.
e. You cannot leave _____ your room is tidy.
f. The match was still played _____ it was raining heavily.

85

© P. Clutterbuck, Good Grammar! Book 3. This page may be reproduced for classroom use.

Conjunctions

Name _____ Grammar BLM

Conjunctions are joining words. They are used to join words and groups of words.

1. Join the sentences using the given conjunction to begin the new sentence.

a. We saw the bully coming. We began to run. (**when**)

_____

b. John did not try very hard. He did not pass the test. (**because**)

_____

c. You help me clean the room. I cannot come out to play. (**unless**)

_____

d. It was very hot. We still played cricket. (**although**)

_____

e. Tom boarded the school bus. He carried his skateboard. (**as**)

_____

2. Choose a word from the box to join the sentences. You might need to change the word order to make the new sentence.

because	although	until

a. The older boys arrive. We can do no more.

_____

b. The tree was not watered. It died last week.

_____

c. We still won the match. Our best player was missing.

_____

d. I will not give you any lollies. You behave.

_____

e. The wheat crops were ruined. It hailed last week.

_____

© P. Clutterbuck, Good Grammar! Book 3. This page may be reproduced for classroom use.

Conjunctions

Name _____ **Grammar BLM**

Conjunctions are joining words. They are used to join words and groups of words.

1. Use a conjunction from the box to complete each sentence.

as	since	unless	but	because
if	although	and	until	when

a. I had not seen her _____ the middle of the year.

b. Sally could not come to the disco _____ she was feeling ill.

c. The weather was cold _____ it was the middle of winter.

d. We left the classroom _____ the bell began to ring.

e. I swept the floor _____ Tom set the table.

f. Our teacher will not help _____ you try hard.

g. Let's sit on the verandah _____ the sun sets.

h. We won the match _____ we were two players short.

i. Jon tried to kick a goal _____ he missed.

j. We must go indoors _____ it begins to rain.

2. Choose your own conjunction to join the sentence in the box to each sentence below.

> Tommy stole the pie.

a. He was feeling hungry.

_____

b. He also stole a gold watch.

_____

c. He was left alone in the kitchen.

_____

d. He did not touch the cakes.

_____

e. He had never stolen anything before.

_____

© P. Clutterbuck, Good Grammar! Book 3. This page may be reproduced for classroom use.

Conjunctions

Conjunctions are joining words. They are used to join words and groups of words.

1. Choose a pair of conjunctions from the box to complete each sentence.

> both . . . and   as . . . as   either . . . or   whether . . . or
> not only . . . but also   neither . . . nor

a. You can have_____ eggs_____ bacon for breakfast.

b. She is_____ tall_____ short.

c. Her brother is _____ handsome_____ intelligent.

d. _____it grows_____ not matters little.

e. Your homework is _____late_____ messy!

f. I will leave_____ soon_____ Ben gets here.

2. Write sentences of your own using the following pairs of conjunctions.

> both . . . and   not . . . but   whether . . . or   not only . . . but also

a. _____

b. _____

c. _____

d. _____

3. Combine the sentences in three different ways, using three different conjunctions. Circle the conjunctions.

a. The freeway was blocked by an accident. The traffic was held up.

_____

_____

_____

b. It was too cold to play outside. We looked over our sticker collections.

_____

_____

© P. Clutterbuck, Good Grammar! Book 3. This page may be reproduced for classroom use.

Sentences

Introduction

A **sentence** is a group of words that makes sense and contains a verb. Take the example, *into the box.* This is not a sentence as it does not have a verb and does not make sense by itself. A sentence begins with a capital letter and ends with a full stop, question mark or exclamation mark.

There are four types of sentences.

(a) **Statements**, which simply state something or give information about something. Examples:

> *It is hot.*
> *The time is eight o'clock.*
> *Koalas are marsupials.*

(b) **Questions**, which ask something. Examples:

> *What is the weather like?*
> *What time is it?*
> *What is a koala?*

(c) **Commands** or **requests**, which direct someone to do something. They can also give advice or warnings. Examples:

> *Get out your books.*
> *Sit up.*
> *Look out for sharp stones.*

(d) **Exclamations**, which express the strong feeling of the speaker or writer about something.

> *Ouch!*
> *I did it!*
> *What a fun day!*

Sentences can take several forms.

(a) **Simple sentences** consist of one clause. They can be divided into two parts: the **subject**, which tells who or what did something, and the **predicate**, which contains the verb and tells us what the subject did or is doing. Examples:

> *Horses (subject) run (predicate).*
> *Billy (subject) climbed the tree (predicate).*

• Sometimes a sentence does not seem to have a subject. Example:

> *Come here!*

In this case, even though the word is not actually said, the speaker is referring to *you.* They are really saying, *(You) come here!* The subject is understood.

(b) **Complex sentences** have more than one verb and thus have more than one clause. A complex sentence has at least one **main clause** (independent clause) and one or more **subordinate clauses** (dependent clauses). Example:

> *When it was hot we went for a swim because we wanted to get cool.*

(c) **Compound sentences** consist of two or more main clauses (independent clauses) joined by a conjunction. Example:

> *I washed the dishes and Billy dried them.*

Speech can be reported directly or indirectly.

(a) **Direct speech** is the exact words spoken by a person. It is usually enclosed in inverted commas. Example:

> *"I am writing a story," said Meg.*

Notice the inverted commas before the first word spoken and those after the last word spoken.

Now look at this sentence.

> *Mike said, "Look at this large dog."*

Here the unspoken words come first. Notice that the first word spoken begins with a capital letter.

The unspoken words can also come between the spoken words. This is sometimes called a broken quotation. Example:

> *"Come close to the fire," said Mike, "and warm your hands."*

Notice two pairs of quotation marks are used.

(b) **Indirect speech** reports a person's speech but does not necessarily quote the exact words used. Example:

> Direct speech: *"I am coming," said Paul.*
> Indirect Speech: *Paul said that he was coming.*

Teaching Strategies

Complete the sentence

Have children add words to complete a sentence. Informal exercises such as this demonstrate to children that a sentence must express a complete thought.

Bill has a new.

I a rabbit.

Jumbled sentences

Write a series of jumbled sentences on the chalkboard. Challenge children to orally unjumble them. As children become more confident, try giving longer sentences.

lives dog a kennel in a

Interview

Choose a volunteer to imagine that they have just returned from the moon. Have the rest of the class imagine that they are reporters and ask suitable questions which the moon traveller must answer in complete sentences.
Is the surface of the moon dry?
How long did it take you to get to the moon?
Select other volunteers to take on other roles for the class to question, for example film star, cricketer, prime minister.

Complete the sentence

Have children complete sentences that you have begun or begin sentences that you have finished. Activities such as this help children understand that sentences have a part that tells who or what did something and a part that tells what they did.
A spider climbed . . .
A dog chased . . .
 . . . swam across the creek.
 . . . bit the boy on the leg.

What am I?

Read a description of an object and ask children to guess what it is. Point out the statements and question in the description, and ask children to answer with a complete sentence. Challenge children to make up their own 'What am I?' statements and questions.
I am small.
I have wings.
I am an insect.
I make honey.
What am I?
I am a bee.

Make the opposite

Write a sentence on the chalkboard. Have children rearrange the words to make the sentence mean the opposite.
The bull chased the boy.   *The boy chased the bull.*

Addo

Call out one word. Children must then add one word at a time to build up a long, sensible sentence. This can be played as a circle game.
Bill
Bill ran
Bill ran across
Bill ran across the . . . and so on.

Subject/predicate match

On separate pieces of cards, write suitable subjects and predicates. Shuffle them and have children make sentences. Children can also make sets of cards for other groups to match.

The dog   are in the garden.
The girls   is climbing the trees.
The boy   is chewing its bone.

Sentence search

Have children search through a text to find:
the longest sentence
the shortest sentence
a question
an exclamation
a command
a statement
direct speech
indirect speech . . .

Make a sentence

Have children make up their own sentences from given words.
farmer   sheep   paddock
The farmer drove the sheep into the paddock.

Find the subject

Give children the opportunity to find the 'hidden' subject of given sentences. This will help them to realise that sentences can be written in different ways.
The girl raced across the lawn.
Across the lawn raced the girl.
Remind students that the easiest way to find the subject is to first locate the verb and then ask who or what is performing that action.

Sentences

A sentence is a group of words that expresses a complete thought. A sentence must make sense and must contain a verb.

1. After each of the following write *yes* if it expresses a complete thought. Write *no* if it does not express a complete thought.

a. With both fists. _____
b. The boy chased the dog. _____
c. In the middle of Australia. _____
d. Dogs bark loudly. _____
e. All her lunch. _____

f. The boys went to the circus. _____
g. On top of the cupboard. _____
h. If you drink that tea. _____
i. One day in July. _____
j. Mike caught three fish. _____

2. Rearrange the words to make correct sentences.

a. bones to likes my dog chew

_____

b. a rose Ali picked the garden in

_____

c. a mammal whale is a

_____

d. weekend we camping are this going

_____

3. Add words of your own to make each of the following a complete sentence.

a. A koala can quickly.

_____

b. The pilot the plane.

_____

c. Have a new.

_____

d. The dog a bone.

_____

© P. Clutterbuck, Good Grammar! Book 3. This page may be reproduced for classroom use.

Sentences

A sentence has a part that tells who or what did something (subject) and a part that tells what they did (predicate).

1. Add a subject to complete each sentence.

a. The_____ made its nest in the tall tree.

b. A large _____ chased the rabbit into its burrow.

c. Beside the house grew large_____ .

d. The little_____ ran happily across the playground.

e. Along the valley stretched the large _____ .

f. _____ inserted fifty cents into the machine.

2. Add a predicate to complete each sentence.

a. The unhappy girl _____.

b. A large eagle _____.

c. The Murray River _____.

d. Cows _____.

e. My new shoes _____.

f. Many trees _____.

3. Draw a line to match each subject to its predicate.

a. The brave fireman   was a famous bushranger.

b. All of the water   were herded into the yards.

c. Gold   rescued the children from the burning house.

d. Ned Kelly   has evaporated.

e. The buffaloes   is mined in many parts of Victoria.

f. The beautiful necklace   are found in Egypt.

g. The pyramids   are native to Australia.

h. Kangaroos and wallabies   was made of silver.

94

© P. Clutterbuck, Good Grammar! Book 3. This page may be reproduced for classroom use.

Sentences

There are four types of sentences: statements, questions, commands or requests, and exclamations.

1. After each sentence, write statement, question, command or exclamation.

a. Where did John go?_____

b. What a lovely day!_____

c. Sit up!_____

d. A magpie is black and white. _____

e. I lost my wallet yesterday. _____

f. Move that chair please._____

g. Why did the bell ring early?_____

h. It's hot!_____

2. **Write different types of sentences.**

a. Write 2 statements about school.

_____

_____

b. Write 2 questions you would like to ask an alien.

_____

_____

c. Write 2 commands you might give a pet.

_____

_____

d. Write 2 exclamations you might make at a football match.

_____

_____

© P. Clutterbuck, Good Grammar! Book 3. This page may be reproduced for classroom use.

Sentences

Name _____   Grammar BLM **55**

There are four types of sentences: statements, questions, commands or requests, and exclamations.

1. Write a possible question to match each answer statement.

a. _____
   It is black and white.

b. _____
   It is nearly seven o'clock.

c. _____
   A beetle has six legs.

d. _____
   The smallest bird is the humming bird.

e. _____
   His name is Rover.

f. _____
   There are twenty-two children.

2. Write a statement to answer each question.

a. What colour is a penguin?
   _____

b. Where do you live?
   _____

c. When do the next holidays begin?
   _____

d. What is a seagull?
   _____

e. What is your favourite animal?
   _____

f. Where is the city of Seoul?
   _____

96

© P. Clutterbuck, Good Grammar! Book 3. This page may be reproduced for classroom use.

Sentences

A simple sentence is made up of one clause. It contains a verb and makes sense on its own. A compound sentence is made up of two or more main clauses joined by a conjunction.
Simple sentence: *I washed the dishes.*
Compound sentence: *I washed the dishes and Bill dried them.*

1. Rewrite each pair of simple sentences as a compound sentence.

a. Mike tried to rescue his dog from the pool. Mike fell in.

_____

b. John switched on the oven. He made a cake.

_____

c. Sam went to the beach. She did not go for a swim.

_____

d. Mum cut the lawn. I raked up the clippings.

_____

2. Add another main clause to make a compound sentence.

a. Sally went to the beach but _____ .
b. A terrier won first prize and_____ .
c. You can go to the movies or_____ .
d. The pies are popular and _____ .

3. Circle the two main clauses in each of these compound sentences.

a. Mike tried to jump the fence but he slipped and fell.

b. Mr Smith lives in Sydney and he also has a horse in Melbourne.

c. Mike and Terry went into the garden and they picked some flowers.

d. You can have a pie or you can have a pizza.

© P. Clutterbuck, Good Grammar! Book 3. This page may be reproduced for classroom use.

Sentences

Name _____   **Grammar BLM**

A simple sentence is made up of one clause. It contains a verb and makes sense on its own.
I washed the dishes.
A compound sentence is made up of two or more main clauses joined by a conjunction.
I washed the dishes and Bill dried them.
A complex sentence is made up of a main clause and a subordinate or dependent clause.
I saw the lady who broke the eggs.

1. Write simple, compound or complex after each sentence.

a. I found my bathers and I went to the pool.   _____

b. We must wait here until the rain stops.   _____

c. The winning girl accepted the prize.   _____

d. Mike found his pencils but he did not find his pens.   _____

e. The concert was held in the old hall.   _____

f. Sam and Joe did not come because they were feeling ill. _____

2. Complete these complex sentences.

a. The farmer did not harvest the crop _____ .

b. We stayed with John _____ .

c. The girl_____ is my best friend.

d. Peter visited the farm _____ .

e. I saw the man_____ .

f. We did not go swimming_____ .

g. There is the dog_____ .

h. The boy _____ catches my bus.

© P. Clutterbuck, Good Grammar! Book 3. This page may be reproduced for classroom use.

Sentences

Direct speech is the exact words spoken by a person. The words are usually enclosed in inverted commas.
"I am writing a story," said Meg.
Indirect speech reports a person's speech but does not necessarily quote the exact words used. The words are not enclosed in inverted commas.
Paul said that he was coming.

1. Add the correct punctuation to show direct speech.

a. Have you been to Melbourne asked Bill.

b. Come and help me shouted Sam.

c. The trip was tiring he said I was glad when I arrived.

d. It's nearly lunchtime shouted Mum. We'll have some fish and chips.

e. You can travel all the way by bus the teacher told us and the scenery is beautiful.

f. Tom said We should leave before six o'clock.

2. Rewrite each sentence as indirect speech.

a. "I would like to go on a picnic," said Tom.

   _____

b. "Where are we going?" asked Kate.

   _____

c. "What time is it?" inquired Fred.

   _____

d. "I can't wait for Christmas," she said.

   _____

e. I asked, "How far is the river from here?"

   _____

f. "Are they going with us?" she asked.

   _____

© P. Clutterbuck, Good Grammar! Book 3. This page may be reproduced for classroom use.

Phrases

Introduction

A **phrase** is a group of words that has no finite verb. Most sentences contain a phrase, although they don't have to. Phrases add meaning and interest to a sentence.

There are different types of phrases that may do the same work as a part of speech.

(a) **Adjectival phrases** tell us more about or describe a noun or pronoun. They should be placed close to the noun they are describing. Example:

> The girl *with long hair* is coming to the party.

(b) **Adverbial phrases** do the work of an adverb. They tell us more about the action of the verb. They tell how, when or where an action happens. Examples:

> The boy kicked the ball *with a lot of skill*. (how)
> Sally will arrive *in a little while*. (when)
> I saw her *near the pool*. (where)

(c) **Noun phrases** do the work of a noun—they name something. Example:

> The *result of the test* is still not known.

Teaching Strategies

Circle the phrases

Have children search through a photocopy of a familiar story to find and circle the phrases. They could colour code the circles to identify the phrases as adjectival, adverbial or noun.

Suggest a phrase

Have children suggest adverbial or adjectival phrases to complete sentences.
The school bell rings *at nine o'clock*.
I saw the girl *with red hair*.

Add a phrase

Have children add phrases of their own to make sentences more interesting.
We left the house.   *We left the house before noon.*
The girl fed the puppy.   *The girl with red hair fed the puppy.*

Where should the phrase go?

Make up a number of sentences in which the phrase has been incorrectly placed. Have children rewrite the sentence correctly.

Phrases

Name _____   Grammar BLM 59

A phrase is a group of words that has no finite verb (a verb with its subject).

1. Write sentences of your own that begin or end with these phrases.

a. On a hot day _____ .

b. After the grape harvest _____ .

c. Near the deserted town _____ .

d. _____ until the bell rings.

e. _____ with lots of courage.

f. _____ just before daylight.

2. Draw a line to match the phrases that have a similar meaning.

a. slow but steady   in the rear

b. very much excited   in a frightened manner

c. after twelve o'clock   before noon

d. with fear and trembling   by gradual degrees

e. at the back   in the afternoon

f. during the morning   without sight

g. unable to see   in a frenzy

3. Draw a line to match the phrases that have opposite meanings.

a. after twelve o'clock   in the background

b. in the classroom   in a cowardly way

c. with great courage   before the sowing

d. after the harvest   slow and sure

e. at great speed   in the playground

f. on the front lawn   in the morning

g. for several hours   only a split second

© P. Clutterbuck, Good Grammar! Book 3. This page may be reproduced for classroom use.

Phrases

A phrase is a group of words that has no finite verb (a verb with its subject). Some phrases do the work of an adjective. They describe or add meaning to a noun.
The girl <u>with red hair</u> is my sister.

1. Circle the adjective phrase in each sentence.

a. The dog with long ears is mine.

b. The man with a guilty conscience is unhappy.

c. The spire on the old church was damaged by the wind.

d. The house on the hill belongs to us.

e. The girl in the green dress is my sister.

f. That table in the kitchen is old.

2. Circle the noun each underlined phrase describes.

a. The aircraft <u>with black wings</u> is above us.

b. The child <u>running across the yard</u> is my nephew.

c. That building <u>near the cliff</u> is falling down.

d. The house <u>in the valley</u> is made of pine logs.

e. The skyscraper <u>in this street</u> was built by my uncle.

f. The church <u>with the cross</u> was built last year.

3. Write an adjective phrase to describe each noun.

a. the cat _____

b. the whale _____

c. the classroom _____

d. the teacher _____

e. the sandwich _____

f. the schoolbag _____

© P. Clutterbuck, Good Grammar! Book 3. This page may be reproduced for classroom use.

Phrases

Name _____ Grammar BLM **61**

A phrase is a group of words that has no finite verb (a verb with its subject). Some phrases do the work of an adverb. They tell how, when or where an action happens.
We walked <u>into the classroom</u>.

1. Circle the adverb phrase in each sentence.

a. We are going to England on Sunday.
b. The watchmaker worked with great care.
c. I put the toys in the box.
d. She spoke in an angry way.
e. I held the injured bird in my hand.
f. After a short pause we continued the search.

2. Circle the action each underlined phrase tells more about.

a. Dad went for a walk <u>to stretch his legs</u>.
b. The boy ran quickly <u>to get to the city</u>.
c. I got some water <u>to have a drink</u>.
d. I got into bed <u>to have a sleep</u>.
e. I listened to the radio <u>to hear the news</u>.
f. We pushed the button <u>to sound the alarm</u>.

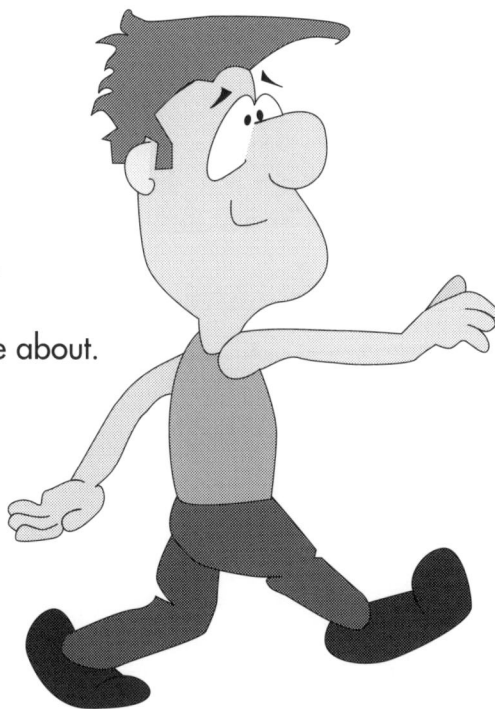

3. Write an adverb phrase to complete each sentence. Each phrase should answer the question in brackets.

a. We saw the birds_____ . (where?)
b. I threw the stone _____ . (why?)
c. Last Saturday we walked _____ . (where?)
d. We left the movies_____ . (when?)
e. The motorist drove _____ . (how?)
f. The teacher spoke to me_____ . (how?)

103

© P. Clutterbuck, Good Grammar! Book 3. This page may be reproduced for classroom use.

Phrases

A phrase is a group of words that has no finite verb (a verb with its subject). Some phrases do the work of a noun.
They name something or answer the what? after the verb.
I have forgotten <u>the name of the boy</u>.

1. Underline the verb in each sentence. Then circle the noun phrase in each sentence.

a. I cannot remember the name of this street.

b. The result of the match is not known yet.

c. The time of the murder was about midnight.

d. Do you know how to get there?

e. I have forgotten the title of the book.

f. The latest news is very worrying.

g. Have you heard the latest news?

2. Choose a noun from the box to replace each noun phrase.

> fist   model   timber   jewel   loam   crumbs   ledge

a. I bought some <u>wood for building</u>. _____

b. We made a <u>very small copy</u>. _____

c. Tom held up a <u>closed hand</u>. _____

d. I threw the <u>bits of bread</u> to the birds. _____

e. The <u>narrow shelf</u> runs along the cliff. _____

f. The <u>rich soil</u> is in the garden. _____

g. The <u>precious stone</u> was stolen. _____

© P. Clutterbuck, Good Grammar! Book 3. This page may be reproduced for classroom use.

Clauses

Introduction

A clause is a group of words that contains a verb and its subject (a finite verb). The subject of a clause may be expressed or understood. In the example, *Stand up!* the subject *you* is understood.

There are two types of clauses.
(a) A **main clause** (independent clause) contains the main thought of the sentence and makes sense standing alone. Examples:
> *I spoke to the teacher* who is our football coach.
> *The dog* that was barking *chased me across the lawn.*
(b) A **subordinate clause** (dependent clause) cannot make sense standing on its own. To make a sentence, subordinate clauses must be added to a main clause. Examples:
> I saw the dog *when I came home.*
> They went to the shop *so they could buy ice-creams.*

Subordinate clauses add information to a sentence and function in the same way as **adjectives**, **adverbs** or **nouns**. Examples:
> That's the house *where Susan lives.* (adjective)
> She didn't want to visit *where Susan lives.* (adverb)
> I don't know *where Susan lives.* (noun)

Sentences are analysed by finding and naming the clauses.
(a) **Simple sentences** consist of one clause. Example:
> *Horses run.*
(b) **Complex sentences** have more than one verb and thus have more than one clause. A complex sentence has at least one main clause (independent clause) and one or more subordinate clauses (dependent clauses). Example:
> *When it was hot we went for a swim because we wanted to get cool.*
(c) **Compound sentences** consist of two or more main clauses (independent clauses) joined by a conjunction. Example:
> *I washed the dishes and Billy dried them.*

See the chapter on conjunctions for more information.

Teaching Strategies

The main thing

Provide students with practice in finding the main clause in a sentence by having them search through a photocopy of a familiar story, circling the main clauses. Remind them that a main clause can stand alone and contains the main thought of the sentence. Point out that a simple sentence is, in fact, one main clause.

Main clause beep

Have children sit in a circle. Choose a child to say a word to start a clause. Each child in turn then adds a word to build a main clause. When the clause is complete, the next child says *beep*. The game can be extended to add a subordinate clause to the main clause.

Act the clause

Organise children in groups of four. Tell groups that the first child is to provide a verb, the second child is to provide a subject, the third child is to arrange the verb and subject to make a clause, and the fourth child is to act out the clause. Ensure that all children get a turn in each role.

Clause match-up

Have children match main clauses to subordinate clauses. This is also an excellent reading activity.

These are the brave boys	*because he was feeling ill.*
Bill did not come	*where the bus stop was.*
The bus driver didn't know	*who rescued the drowning child.*

Clause call-out

Write a main clause on the chalkboard and challenge children to call out appropriate subordinate clauses.

We went to the park	*when we had eaten lunch.*
	where the banksia tree grows.
	because we wanted to play.

Verb search

Write some clauses on the chalkboard. Have children search for and identify the verbs in each clause.

I saw the boy who broke the glass.

Add the verb

Have children orally add missing verbs to clauses.

I saw the boy who ten goals.
I saw the boy who kicked ten goals.
The police arrested the thief who the jewels.
The police arrested the thief who stole the jewels.

Clauses

A clause is a group of words that contains a verb and its subject. A main clause contains the main thought of the sentence and makes sense standing alone. A subordinate clause (dependent clause) does not make sense standing on its own. It adds information to the sentence.

1. Draw a line to match each main clause to its subordinate clause.

Main clause	Subordinate clause
a. Where is the book	where the railway station was.
b. Here is the burglar	if we get any hail.
c. I asked the stranger	because her uncle has arrived.
d. The grape crop will be damaged	which has yellow blossoms over it.
e. Winter is the season	that I read yesterday?
f. Sally would not come with us	whose dog bit the policeman.
g. I know the man	who was arrested by the police.
h. This is the tree	when the snow begins to fall.

2. Underline the main clause and circle the subordinate clause in each sentence. Hint! The main clause might be in two parts with the subordinate clause embedded in between.

a. The student who stayed away from school was punished.

b. The lady who is in charge of the school spoke to the grade 3 teachers.

c. I broke the bottle that had juice in it.

d. The farm where the grapes are grown belongs to my uncle.

e. The shed that houses the equipment was burnt to the ground.

f. The cupboard that is used to store glasses is made of mahogany.

g. The food that is fit to be eaten is in the refrigerator.

h. We visited the place where stone is mined.

© P. Clutterbuck, Good Grammar! Book 3. This page may be reproduced for classroom use.

Clauses

Name _____ **Grammar BLM** **64**

A clause is a group of words that contains a verb and its subject.
Subordinate clauses add information to a sentence and function in the
same way as adjectives, adverbs or nouns.
That's the house *where Susan lives.* (adjective)
She didn't want to visit *where Susan lives.* (adverb)
I don't know *where Susan lives.* (noun)

1. Draw lines to match each main clause with an adjective subordinate clause.

    a. The farmer shot the dogs   which began on Christmas Day

    b. Our holiday . . . was very restful.   which likes to chase its tail.

    c. We admired the garden   whose father comes from England.

    d. I spoke to the boy   that killed the sheep.

    e. I have a new puppy   which is in the museum

    f. The dinosaur . . . was found by Sam.   which we had planted in spring.

2. Complete each sentence by adding an adjective subordinate clause.

    a. This is the girl <u>who</u> _____ .

    b. The old cow <u>which</u> _____looked sick.

    c. The picture <u>which</u> _____ was painted by my friend.

    d. The old lady <u>who</u> _____ makes great pizzas.

    e. The brave girl <u>who</u> _____ was awarded a medal.

    f. I caught the robber <u>that</u> _____ .

3. Complete each sentence by adding an adjective subordinate clause.

    a. Sally found a wallet_____ .

    b. We switched off the music_____ .

    c. I showed John the knife _____ .

    d. I told her to throw away the shirt _____ .

108

© P. Clutterbuck, Good Grammar! Book 3. This page may be reproduced for classroom use.

Clauses

A clause is a group of words that contains a verb and its subject.
Subordinate clauses add information to a sentence and function in the same way as adjectives, adverbs or nouns.
That's the house *where Susan lives*. (adjective)
She didn't want to visit *where Susan lives*. (adverb)
I don't know *where Susan lives*. (noun)

1. Circle the verb that each underlined subordinate clause tells us more about.

a. She can climb a tree <u>as a monkey does</u>.

b. I punished Spot <u>because he chewed my new shoe</u>.

c. Meet me <u>where the water pipe burst</u>.

d. <u>After we have had lunch</u> we are going to the movies.

e. No spectators are allowed <u>while a rehearsal is in progress</u>.

f. They were asleep <u>before the sun had set</u>.

2. Underline the adverb subordinate clause in each sentence. On the line, write whether it tells us how, when or why the action of the verb took place.

a. I went swimming because it was hot.   _____

b. The girls played where there were trees.   _____

c. You may dress as you wish.   _____

d. We left the classroom when the bell rang.   _____

e. As our captain is sick we must choose another player.   _____

f. Accidents often happen where two roads cross each other.   _____

3. Draw a line to match each main clause with an adverb subordinate clause.

a. We must play inside   because he could not find his uniform.

b. John spoke   where the roads meet.

c. Mike did not come   since she left to live in the city.

d. I haven't seen Janet   when he was a small child.

e. We must leave the dishes   until the rain stops.

f. The accident happened   as if he was very nervous.

109

© P. Clutterbuck, Good Grammar! Book 3. This page may be reproduced for classroom use.

Clauses

A clause is a group of words that contains a verb and its subject.
Subordinate clauses add information to a sentence and function in the
same way as adjectives, adverbs or nouns.
That's the house *where Susan lives.* (adjective)
She didn't want to visit *where Susan lives.* (adverb)
I don't know *where Susan lives.* (noun)

1. Look at each underlined subordinate clause. Write whether it is an adjective clause, an adverb clause or a noun clause.

a. The cup <u>that is on the shelf</u> belongs to Tom.   _____

b. <u>What he said</u> is truly a lie.   _____

c. Egypt is a land <u>that has lots of pyramids</u>.   _____

d. Tom did not ride his bike <u>because it had a flat tyre</u>. _____

e. Ned cleaned his teeth <u>after he had eaten</u>.   _____

f. The witness stated <u>that she recognised the man</u>.   _____

g. We left the party <u>when the music began</u>.   _____

h. <u>After they had eaten their lunch</u> they played games. _____

2. Add the type of subordinate clause asked for in brackets.

a. The scouts camped_____. (adverb clause)

b. Australia is a land _____ . (adjective clause)

c. Mike washed his hands_____. (adverb clause)

d. Sally did not come_____. (adverb clause)

e. _____ they played games. (adverb clause)

f. The truth is _____. (noun clause)

g. _____ is not true. (noun clause)

h. The police are searching for a man _____. (adjective clause)

© P. Clutterbuck, Good Grammar! Book 3. This page may be reproduced for classroom use.

Clauses

Name _____

An adjectival clause should be placed next to, or as close as possible to, the noun it is describing.

1. Rewrite each of these sentences so they make more sense.

a. I bought the tiger from the lady <u>that had black and gold stripes</u>.

_____

b. The baby was picked up by the old man <u>who had a dummy in his mouth</u>.

_____

c. The teacher spoke to the little boy <u>who is married with two children</u>.

_____

d. The train is in the station <u>that arrived late</u>.

_____

e. The bull gored the man <u>that has two large horns</u>.

_____

f. In front of the house is an oak tree <u>which has a red roof</u>.

_____

2. Join the two sentences so that the new sentence contains an adjective clause.

a. This is the dog. The dog attacked the stranger.

_____

b. This is the girl. The girl lives next door to me.

_____

c. The children hurried past the old house. The house was said to be haunted.

_____

d. The big gum tree has been cut down. It stood in our backyard.

_____

e. The boy won a silver medal. I knew the boy well.

_____

f. The families were cared for by neighbours. Their homes were destroyed in the bushfires.

_____

© P. Clutterbuck, Good Grammar! Book 3. This page may be reproduced for classroom use.

Clauses

Sentences can have more than one subordinate clause.

1. Use the following clauses to complete the sentences below. Write the number in the space.

    1 who caught the thief
    2 where the thief had hidden them

    3 that had broken a wing
    4 that was growing in our backyard

    5 who was playing cricket
    6 when the ball hit him

    7 who were unarmed
    8 that were very hungry

    9 who live in our street
    10 that my father drives

    11 who was sitting in the front seat
    12 where he could leave his bag

    a. I found the bird _____ in a tall tree _____ .
    b. The hunters _____ were attacked by wolves _____ .
    c. The policeman _____ found the jewels _____ .
    d. Tom _____ asked the teacher _____ .
    e. The boy _____ hurt his head _____ .
    f. Many people _____ like the car _____ .

2. Complete each sentence by adding clauses of your own. The words to begin each clause are given.

    a. The man <u>who</u> _____ fell <u>when</u> _____ .
    b. The river <u>that</u> _____ was swum by the girl <u>who</u> _____ .
    c. The birds <u>that</u> _____ were shot by the hunter <u>who</u> _____ .
    d. The boy <u>who</u> _____ did not play <u>because</u> _____ .
    e. The girls <u>who</u> _____ waited <u>until</u> _____ .
    f. The footballer <u>whose</u> _____ kicked the goal <u>that</u> ___ _____ .
    g. The teacher <u>who</u> _____ laughed <u>when</u> _____ .

© P. Clutterbuck, Good Grammar! Book 3. This page may be reproduced for classroom use.

Punctuation

Introduction

An easy way to draw children's attention to the importance of punctuation is to make an analogy to the road signs we must obey. *A stop sign signals to a motorist that she must stop and not proceed until everything is clear. A full stop tells us we must stop a moment so that sentences do not run into each other and become difficult to understand. A give way sign tells a motorist to pause to ensure the traffic has passed. A comma tells us to pause to ensure the sentence makes sense. If all motorists obey the traffic signs then cars, trucks and bikes will travel along streets safely. If we all obey the punctuation signals then we will be able to convey our thoughts and ideas clearly.*

The main elements of punctuation that Upper Primary children should develop a working knowledge of are as follows.

A **capital letter** is used:
(a) for the first letter of a sentence
(b) for the first letter of a person's given name and family name
(c) for the pronoun I
(d) for the first letter of names of the days of the week, months of the year and special times such as *Easter, Christmas*
(e) for the first letter of names of towns, cities, countries, streets, schools, etc.
(f) sometimes to begin each line in poetry
(g) for the first letter of the main words in the titles of books, poems, songs and television programs

A **full stop** is used:
(a) at the end of a statement or command sentence. Examples:
   That dog is brown. (statement)
   Sit down. (command)
(b) in abbreviations if the first letter and only part of the word is used. Examples:
   etcetera   etc.
   Captain   Capt.
   Crescent   Cres.
However if the last letter is included in the abbreviation, no full stop is used. Examples:
   Mister   Mr

Doctor	*Dr*
Road	*Rd*

A **question mark** is used at the end of a sentence that is a direct question. It might be helpful to point out the question indicators *who, when, where, why, what* and *how.*

> *What is the time?* (direct question)
> *I asked her what time it was.* (indirect question)

An **exclamation mark** is used at the end of a sentence that expresses a strong emotion. Point out to children that exclamation sentences are often short. Examples:

> *Wow!   Ouch!   Well done!*

Remind children to only use one exclamation mark. Using more than one does not create greater emphasis.

A **comma** is used:

(a) to separate words in a list. Examples:
> *Please go to the store and buy oranges, bread, milk and butter.* (separate nouns)
> *It was a big, black, hairy spider.* (separate adjectives)
> *Please work quickly, neatly and quietly.* (separate adverbs)

(b) after the salutation in a letter. Example:
> *Dear Katy,*

(c) at the end of a letter, before signing your name. Example:
> *Yours faithfully,*

(d) to separate direct speech from the rest of the sentence. Example:
> *"I hope he will be here soon," said Mike.*

(e) to separate two or more adjectives or adverbs. Examples:
> *Susan is a fast, accurate, cheerful worker.*
> *The cat slowly, silently, skilfully moved in on the mouse.*

(f) sometimes to separate a connective from the rest of the sentence if the connective is used to begin the sentence. Example:
> *So, they went to the movies in the afternoon.*

(g) sometimes to separate a beginning phrase or clause from the rest of the sentence. Example:
> *In the cool of the evening, we will have a picnic in the park.*

(h) to separate embedded phrases and clauses from the rest of the sentence. Example:
> *Ms Jackson, our new music teacher, used to play in a band.*

(i) when punctuating direct speech. See the chapter on sentences for more information about direct speech.

Inverted commas are used to enclose direct speech (the words actually spoken by someone). Examples:

> *Ali asked, "When are we going?"*
> *"Let's go now," said Ben.*

See the chapter on sentences for more information about direct speech.

An **apostrophe** is used:

(a) in contractions to indicate where letters have been omitted. Example:

> *I will   I'll*

(b) to indicate possession in nouns. Examples:

> *a dog's kennel*
> *the three dogs' kennels*

This area must be treated with great care. Children tend to add apostrophes incorrectly—usually when making plural endings.

A **dash** is used:

(a) to mark a change of thought or an abrupt turn in the sentence, or to indicate faltering speech. Example:

> *You can't do that—oh, you can.*

(b) to indicate an unfinished or interrupted sentence. Example:

> *But, Sir I thought—*

(c) to enclose extra information. (Brackets can also be used for this. However brackets must come in pairs.) Example:

> *Somewhere in Australia—I'm not sure of the exact spot—is a large deposit of gold.*

A **colon** is used to introduce more information. The information may be: a list, words, phrases, clauses or a quotation. Examples:

> *He bought lots of fruit including: apples, pineapple, watermelon and bananas.*

A **semicolon** is used:

(a) to join two short linked sentences. Example:

> *I like jelly; my sister prefers ice-cream.*

(b) to separate complex lists. Example:

> *With her she brought a jacket with a hood; a coat with big pockets, a fur collar and a matching scarf; and a large umbrella.*

(c) sometimes at the ends of lines of poetry.

A **hyphen** is used:

(a) to form compound adjectives. Example:

> *the blackish-blue fish*

(b) when the main word starts with a capital letter. Example:
> *un-Australian*

(c) to avoid confusion with another word. Example:
> *re-cover (fit with a new cover)*
> *recover (return to normal)*

These are just some of the uses of the hyphen. There are no firm rules about their use so it's best to check in a dictionary if you are unsure.

Teaching Strategies

Beep marks
Make cards that have large punctuation marks written on them. Read a simple story aloud to the children. Whenever you reach a punctuation mark say, 'Beep!'. The children must then hold up the missing mark.

What's the meaning?
From time to time challenge children by writing a piece on the chalkboard in which the meaning may be altered by incorrect punctuation.

Have you eaten Bill?	*Have you eaten, Bill?*
I have forty-two dollar coins.	*I have forty two-dollar coins.*
Sally is a pretty, kind person.	*Sally is a pretty kind person.*
He ate a half-fried chicken.	*He ate a half fried chicken.*
I left him convinced he was a fool.	*I left him, convinced he was a fool.*

What a joke
Give children plenty of practice punctuating by writing unpunctuated jokes or riddles on the chalkboard. Have individual children add the punctuation in colour.
what cat lives in the sea
an octopus

Read aloud
Have individual children read aloud their own writing efforts while other children suggest punctuation necessary.

Punctuation

Name _____ Grammar BLM **69**

A capital letter is used for:
• **the first letter of a sentence.**
• **the first letter in names—books, plays, poems, films, songs, people, places, pets, days, months, countries, states, towns, mountains, rivers.**
• **the pronoun *I.***

1. Colour the boxes that contain words that should begin with a capital letter.

michelle	wagga wagga	plate	christmas	beetles
south	uranus	october	canada	mount everest
england	asia	pacific ocean	tables	london
wednesday	summer	easter	hobart	rialto house
stranger	shamrock hotel	vietnam	murray river	wattle street

2. Complete the sentences.
a. My given name is _____ .
b. My birthday is in the month of _____ .
c. The street I live in is _____ .
d. The school I attend is _____ .
e. My teacher's name is _____ .
f. I live in the town or city of _____ .
g. The country I would most like to visit is _____ .

3. Rewrite the following sentences correctly.
a. last saturday julie went to melbourne

_____

b. at christmas we are going to italy which is a country in europe

_____

c. the wedding will take place at st patrick's church in greensborough next winter

_____ 117

Punctuation

Name _____ Grammer BLM **70**

Commas are used to show short pauses in writing. They are used in various ways, including: separating nouns, separating adjectives and adverbs, after introductory words, and separating parts of long sentences.

1. Complete each sentence using words from the box. Don't forget to use commas to mark off the separate items.

> scissors   rice   skunk   ash   sycamore   hammer   eucalypt
> wheat   rose   zebra   pliers   daffodil   corn   penguin   hyacinth

a. _____ are cereals.
b. _____ are flowers.
c. _____ are black-and-white.
d. _____ are tools.
e. _____ are trees.

2. Each sentence contains a phrase that needs to be marked off with commas. The first one has been done for you.

a. Adelaide, the capital of South Australia, is a beautiful city.

b. Anders Celsius a Swedish astronomer introduced the centigrade scale in 1742.

c. The South Pole a featureless spot in a freezing wilderness was first reached by Amundsen.

d. The toothbrush according to a 17th century encyclopaedia was first invented in China in 1498.

e. Ian one of this class's finest writers has won first prize in the poetry contest.

f. Interpol the first international crime fighting organisation was formed in 1923 in Paris.

118

© P. Clutterbuck, Good Grammar! Book 3. This page may be reproduced for classroom use.

Punctuation

Name _____ Grammar BLM **71**

An apostrophe is used:
- **in contractions to indicate where letters have been omitted.**
  I'll (I will)
- **to indicate possession in nouns.**
  a dog's kennel
  the three dogs' kennels

1. Write in full what the following contractions mean.

a. hasn't _____   e. we'll _____

b. we've _____   f. can't _____

c. o'clock _____   g. 'tis _____

d. didn't _____   h. 'twas _____

2. Write the following as contractions.

a. I am _____   f. you have _____

b. I have _____   g. who is _____

c. I would _____   h. it is _____

d. I shall _____   i. he is _____

e. could not _____   j. were not _____

3. Add apostrophes where they are needed.

Thats the place well go. Theres bound to be lots of fish. Its a really

good spot. Were lucky youd seen it before. Theyre going to be

jealous when they know weve got it. Theyll probably say theyre

not coming now.

119

© P. Clutterbuck, Good Grammar! Book 3. This page may be reproduced for classroom use.

Punctuation

An apostrophe is used:
- **in contractions to indicate where letters have been omitted.**
  I'll (I will)
- **to indicate possession in nouns.**
  a dog's kennel
  the three dogs' kennels

1. Add apostrophes where they are needed.

a. The policemans helmet fell on the ground.

b. I fastened the dogs collar around its neck.

c. My mothers car is in the garage.

d. The clocks hands pointed to midday.

e. The elephants tusk was taken by the hunter.

f. The childs foot slipped on the step.

2. Add apostrophes where they are needed.

a. The ladies hats are on the bed.

b. The childrens toys are in the box.

c. The cows tails swished about like fly swats.

d. My sisters bedrooms are next to each other.

e. The cities skyscrapers are always a beautiful sight.

f. The eagles beaks were sharp and curved.

3. Rewrite these phrases making use of apostrophes.
   The first one has been done for you.

a. the ears of the horse   the horse's ears _____

b. the boots of the soldier   _____

c. the hats of the men   _____

d. the tail of the tiger   _____

e. the books of the teacher   _____

f. the red noses of the clowns _____

© P. Clutterbuck, Good Grammar! Book 3. This page may be reproduced for classroom use.

Punctuation

Name _____   **Grammar BLM** 73

An exclamation is used at the end of a sentence that expresses a strong emotion. Exclamations are often short.

1. Rewrite the following sentences as exclamations. Use only one, two or three words.

a. The stove is on fire and I am afraid the house might burn down.

_____

b. I want you to be fast.

_____

c. I need your help urgently and straight away.

_____

d. You must hold on tightly or you will be thrown off.

_____

e. You must watch where you are going because a large truck is about to hit you.

_____

f. Our team has just scored a goal.

_____

2. Write exclamation marks, question marks or full stops where they are needed.

a. What a great movie I really like the end What big sharks

b. Did you see the spider Look out There could be one on your hat

c. What a lovely day Look at those waves Wow

d. Yuk How horrible Would you believe it

3. Write exclamations beginning with the following words.

a. How _____

b. What _____

c. If only _____

d. How _____

e. What _____

f. If only _____

121

© P. Clutterbuck, Good Grammar! Book 3. This page may be reproduced for classroom use.

Punctuation

A semicolon is used to join two short linked sentences or to separate complex lists.

1. Add commas or semicolons in the correct places.
   a. It was nearly Christmas so we looked for presents.
   b. I was really exhausted I had never run so far.
   c. Mr Smith is a good teacher however you need to listen to him carefully.
   d. Football is a winter sport cricket is a summer sport.
   e. Lisa was the teacher's first choice she was quiet intelligent and a hard worker.
   f. On our visit to the zoo we saw zebras grazing in a paddock lots of snakes in the snakepit seals their babies and a diver in the pool and a elephant in its enclosure.

A colon is used to introduce more information. The information may be: a list, words, phrases, clauses or a quotation.

2. Add commas or colons in the correct places.
   a. These are my favourite foods hamburgers pies lollies and apples.
   b. This is what he said "The Australian flag is red white and blue."
   c. Get these things books pens papers pencils and crayons.
   d. The instructions read as follows wash lightly in cold water.

A dash is used to mark a change of thought or an abrupt turn in the sentence, to indicate an unfinished or interrupted sentence, or to enclose extra information.

3. Write three sentences of your own in which dashes can be used.

   a. _____

   b. _____

122 c. _____

© P. Clutterbuck, Good Grammar! Book 3. This page may be reproduced for classroom use.

Vocabulary

Introduction

Grammar is also concerned with the way an overall text is structured to engage an audience and to deliver its message, and the way we choose particular words appropriate to that audience and message. It is important to generate an interest in words and to encourage children to be thoughtful about the words they use. If children develop an interest in language at an early age they should continue throughout their school life and into adulthood appreciating the richness and diversity of our ever-growing language.

Concepts Upper Primary children should become familiar with are as follows:

Antonyms

An antonym is a word that has the opposite meaning to another word. Example:

> *Absent/present*

Synonyms

A synonym is a word that has the same or a similar meaning to another word. Help children to understand that writers choose their words carefully and that one word may be more appropriate than another in a given situation. Example:

> *wed/marry*

Homonyms

There are two types.

(a) A **homophone** is a word that sounds the same as another word but has a different meaning and different spelling. Examples:
> *bear/bare*   *sun/son*

(b) A **homograph** is a word that is spelled the same as another word but has a different meaning. Examples:
> *I fished from the bank of the river.*
> *I cashed the cheque at the bank.*
> *I don't think you should bank on it too much.*

Anagrams

An anagram is a word that contains exactly the same letters as another word— but in a different arrangement. Examples:
> *palm/lamp*   *flow/wolf*

Compound words

These are sometimes called joined words. They are simply a large word made up of two or more smaller words. The combinations can be a noun and noun, (shell + fish = shellfish) or an adjective and a noun (black + bird = blackbird).

Twin words

These are words that are often paired together, especially in speech. Example:
> *salt and pepper*

Similes

A simile is a figure of speech that compares one thing with another. It is a direct comparison introduced by the words *like* or *as*. Example:

> *Her hair was like spun gold.*
> *The pavement was as hot as fire.*

Metaphors

A metaphor is an implied comparison. Rather than saying one thing is *like* another, a metaphor says that one thing is another. Example:

> *The clouds were full sacks ready to burst.*

Base words, prefixes and suffixes

It is often helpful to see a word in terms of its various parts. These parts are called the base, the prefix and the suffix.

The **base word** is the word from which other words are built. Example:

> *kind*

A **prefix** is a group of letters placed at the beginning of a word. It often makes the word mean its opposite. Example:

> *un + kind = unkind*

A **suffix** is a group of letters added to the end of a word. (Sometimes spelling changes have to be made.) Example:

unkindly:	*un*	*kind*	*ly*
	prefix	*base*	*suffix*

Teaching Strategies

Homophone hunt

Write a list of words on the chalkboard. Challenge children to think of the corresponding homophones. Children can also create cartoons to illustrate the homophones.

allowed/aloud	*ate/eight*	*eye/I*	*bare/bear*
bean/been	*blew/blue*	*board/bored*	*brake/break*
flea/flee	*hear/here*	*knit/nit*	*one/won*
pair/pear	*sun/son*		

Snap

On blank playing cards write pairs of synonyms, antonyms or homophones. Encourage children to play 'Snap' with them.

Scattered letters

Write a selection of letters scattered on the chalkboard. Have children think of as many words as they can using the letters. Make the game more challenging by introducing a timer.

Word collection

Organise a word collection bulletin board in the classroom. Encourage children to find, collect and then display words on the board. The board could have a number of different headings, such as Interesting Words, Words that Sound Funny, Words that Sound Like Noises, Words that Sound Important. Ask children to think of other headings they would like to use.

Tongue twisters

Challenge children to say a tongue twister quickly. Then have them make up their own tongue twisters for their friends to try.

Odd words

Have children search for words with interesting or unusual features. Here are some to start them off.

hijinks:	*three dotted letters in a row*
strength:	*eight letters but only one vowel*
subbookkeeper:	*four sets of double letters*
facetious:	*all the vowels in their correct order*
cauliflower:	*contains all the vowels*
education:	*contains all the vowels*

Daily letter race

Challenge children to write all the words they can in two minutes that begin with the first letter of that day of the week.

Word link

Have one child say a word. The next child has to respond by saying a word that starts with the letter that the first word ended with. Make the game more or less challenging by setting a rule determining the minimum number of letters or syllables that the words must have, or a specific part of speech.

Rule:	*two or more syllables*
First child:	*humour*
Second child:	*rubble*
Third child:	*elephant*

Continuous story

Divide the class into groups. Have one child in each group start a story by saying one word. The next child in the group then adds another word and so on until the group has word-by-word written a story that makes sense. The group that can go on the longest is the winner.

Word Origins

1. Choose a word from the box to complete each sentence. The Old English root and meaning are given in the brackets.

> witness   barrow   ferry   breakfast   grave   scraped

a. I filled the _____ (bera: to carry) with garden waste.
b. I caught a _____ (faran: to go) to take me across the bay.
c. The _____ (witan: to know) testified that she saw the thief.
d. The small boy _____ (sceran: to cut) his knee when he fell.
e. We discovered the old _____ (grafan: to dig) of an explorer.
f. I like to eat cereal and eggs for my _____ (brecan: to break).

2. Choose a word from the box to complete each sentence. The Latin root and meaning are given in the brackets.

> city   anniversary   current   manufacture   dentist   errors

a. The strong _____ (curro: I run) swept the swimmers away.
b. The _____ (dens: tooth) extracted my teeth.
c. We celebrate our tenth _____ (annus: a year) next Tuesday.
d. Melbourne is a large _____ (civis: citizen).
e. Cars are _____ (manar: a hand) in that factory.
f. Tom made several _____ (erro: I wander) in his spelling.

3. Choose a word from the box to complete each sentence. The Greek root and meaning are given in the brackets.

> autograph   astronomer   perimeter   democratic   photograph

a. I took a _____ (photo: light) of our entire grade.
b. The film star gave me her _____ (autos: self).
c. We have a _____ (demos: people) government in Australia.
d. We measured the _____ (metron: a measure) of the square.
e. The _____ (aster: a star) looked through the telescope.

© P. Clutterbuck, Good Grammar! Book 3. This page may be reproduced for classroom use.

Base Words

A base word is a word from which other words are built.
A prefix is a group of letters placed at the beginning of a word.
A suffix is a group of letters added at the end of a word.

1. Change the order of the following word parts to make the word suggested by the definitions.

   a. able   un   reason   (not fair) _____

   b. suit   able   un   (not good enough) _____

   c. ed   un   want   (not needed) _____

   d. able   en   joy   (lots of fun) _____

   e. ly   in   correct   (not in a correct way) _____

2. Circle the base word in each of the following.

   a. unemployment   f. imprisonment

   b. disrespectful   g. disappearance

   c. dishonourable   h. uncertainty

   d. informally   i. reappearing

   e. unpleasantness   j. reconstruction

3. Think of five words of your own that have a prefix. Then think of five words that have a suffix.

Prefix	Suffix

© P. Clutterbuck, Good Grammar! Book 3. This page may be reproduced for classroom use.

Similes

Name _____ **Grammar BLM** 77

A simile is a figure of speech that compares one thing to another. It is a direct comparison introduced by the words *like* or *as*.

1. Use a word from the box to complete each simile.

> toast   ice   sugar   mouse   rock   feathers

a. as soft as _____
b. as sweet as _____
c. as cold as _____
d. as hard as a _____
e. as warm as _____
f. as small as a _____

2. Use a word from the box to complete each simile.

> silk   bee   kitten   coal   eel   snow

a. The cloth was as black as _____ .
b. The wet ball was as slippery as an _____ .
c. My little sister is as playful as a _____ .
d. The top of this table is as smooth as _____ .
e. I've been as busy as a _____ lately.
f. The lamb is as white as _____ .

3. Add a word of your own to complete each simile. Compare your answers with those of a friend.

a. as wet as _____
b. as big as _____
c. as graceful as _____
d. as hot as _____
e. as tough as _____
f. as gentle as _____

© P. Clutterbuck, Good Grammar! Book 3. This page may be reproduced for classroom use.

Metaphors

Name _____ **Grammar BLM** **78**

A metaphor is more forceful than a simile. Instead of saying that one thing is *like* another, it supposes that one thing *is* another.
Simile: **He is as cunning as a fox.**
Metaphor: **He is a cunning fox.**

1. Condense each simile and rewrite it as a metaphor.

a. You are wasting your time, like a person flogging a dead horse.

_____

b. She is so ill that she seems to have one foot in the grave.

_____

c. We are both sharing the same risks, like two people in the same boat.

_____

d. He is very clumsy, just as though his fingers were all thumbs.

_____

e. I was so disappointed that it seemed as if my heart had broken.

_____

2. Use each word in two sentences—literally in the first, metaphorically in the second.

a. cloud _____

_____

b. forest _____

_____

c. river _____

_____

d. book _____

_____

e. galaxy _____

_____

f. snail _____

_____

129

© P. Clutterbuck, Good Grammar! Book 3. This page may be reproduced for classroom use.

Compound Words

Compound words are made up of two or more smaller words.

1. Add a word from the box to complete each compound word below.

> ache   money   boards   quake   prints   coat   where   fly

a. A severe earth _____ shook the city.

b. The house is made of weather _____ .

c. Sally is given five dollars pocket _____ each week.

d. Tommy has a painful tooth _____ .

e. We could see the butter _____ in the rose bushes.

f. We searched every _____ for the missing money.

g. As it was cold outside, he wore an over _____ .

h. We could see the foot _____ in the snow.

2. Circle the compound words. You should be able to find fifteen.

Mike got the eggcup from the cupboard and placed it on the clean tablecloth. He wanted to eat his breakfast quickly as he was going to play football that day. He always played full-back. When he got to school he put his books inside the classroom and then went out into the playground. Everybody asked him if he had remembered to do his homework. He said that he had done it in a notebook that his grandfather had given him for his birthday.

3. These compound words have been muddled. Write the eight words correctly.

> | raindust | carburger | handshoe | eyeprint |
> | horseshake | cheeseport | sawdrop | fingerbrow |

_____   _____

_____   _____

_____   _____

_____   _____

© P. Clutterbuck, Good Grammar! Book 3. This page may be reproduced for classroom use.

Anagrams

An anagram is a word made by rearranging all the letters of another word.

1. Rearrange the letters of the word to make a new word to match the meaning in the brackets. The first one has been done for you.

   a. sever   (part of a poem)   verse _____

   b. sale   (sea creature)   _____

   c. blow   (dish)   _____

   d. seat   (direction)   _____

   e. lump   (fruit)   _____

   f. sore   (flower)   _____

   g. flow   (farmyard bird)   _____

   h. arts   (rodents)   _____

   i. mean   (hair on a horse's neck)   _____

2. Rearrange the words in brackets to make more suitable words for the story.

   Tom and his best (**meat**)_____Sam were walking through the flower

   (**danger**)_____when they saw a large (**low**)_____ sitting

   on the branch of a (**lamp**)_____tree. Sam said it (**saw**)_____

   the (**seam**)_____one that he had seen (**salt**)_____week.

3. Rearrange the letters of the word in brackets to make a word that completes the sentence.

   a. The meal was served on a china _____. (**petal**)

   b. The _____ is an important organ of the body. (**earth**)

   c. We put the boxes on the kitchen _____. (**bleat**)

   d. After travelling south, the explorers decided to turn_____. (**thorn**)

   e. The teacher told us to be _____. (**tinsel**)

   f. He hurt his _____when he jammed it in the door. (**fringe**)

© P. Clutterbuck, Good Grammar! Book 3. This page may be reproduced for classroom use.

Synonyms

A synonym is a word that has the same or similar meaning to another word.

1. Circle all the words in the grid. Then write each one beside its synonym.

l	a	r	g	e	t	s
s	l	w	c	r	a	h
o	o	a	l	o	s	a
f	s	i	a	a	t	k
t	e	l	p	m	e	e
s	e	r	i	o	u	s
b	r	a	v	e	r	y

a. howl _____

b. wander _____

c. tender _____

d. tremble _____

e. immense _____

f. misplace _____

g. valour _____

h. applaud _____

i. solemn _____

j. flavour _____

2. Each underlined word can be replaced with a synonym from the box. Find and write the word.

wet	ill	fat	old	odd	gem	sly	get

a. We are trying to <u>obtain</u> some money. _____

b. The <u>crafty</u> fox was captured. _____

c. The clothes are still <u>damp</u>. _____

d. Mary is feeling <u>sick</u>. _____

e. The pig is quite <u>plump</u>. _____

f. This seems quite <u>strange</u>. _____

g. This building is <u>ancient</u>. _____

h. The <u>jewel</u> is very valuable. _____

© P. Clutterbuck, Good Grammar! Book 3. This page may be reproduced for classroom use.

Antonyms

An antonym is a word that has the opposite meaning to another word.

1. Circle all the words in the grid. Then write each one beside its antonym.

s	b	u	i	l	d	c
m	c	h	e	a	p	o
i	l	e	a	v	e	w
l	t	i	m	i	d	a
e	s	o	u	t	h	r
l	o	o	s	e	n	d
s	w	a	l	l	o	w
a	w	k	w	a	r	d

a. expensive _____

b. bold _____

c. hero _____

d. north _____

e. demolish _____

f. graceful _____

g. tighten _____

h. return _____

i. frown _____

j. vomit _____

2. Select the word from the box that has the opposite meaning to the underlined word in each sentence.

> solid   divide   smash   light   fake   deceitful   entrance   feeble

a. These books are quite <u>heavy</u>. _____

b. Are you going to <u>repair</u> the motor. _____

c. The teacher told us to <u>multiply</u> the numbers. _____

d. He is a very <u>honest</u> boy. _____

e. We left quickly through the open <u>exit</u>. _____

f. After the operation, she felt quite <u>strong</u>. _____

g. These logs are <u>hollow</u>. _____

h. These diamonds are <u>genuine</u>. _____

133

© P. Clutterbuck, Good Grammar! Book 3. This page may be reproduced for classroom use.

Homophones

A homophone is a word that sounds the same as another word but has a different meaning and different spelling.

1. Circle all the words in the grid. Then write each word beside its homophone.

f	l	a	w	m	m	g	w
v	f	h	b	e	a	u	a
a	i	y	a	d	y	e	i
i	n	m	w	a	o	s	s
n	d	n	l	l	r	t	t
t	a	u	g	h	t	x	x

a. find _____

b. ball _____

c. taut _____

d. floor _____

e. meddle _____

f. waste _____

g. guessed _____

h. him _____

i. vein _____

j. mare _____

2. Circle the correct word in the brackets.

Two (**buoys** **boys**) were walking beside a (**creak** **creek**). They were hoping to (**fined** **find**) (**sum** **some**) (**mail** **male**) (**dear** **deer**) that had (**been** **bean**) seen grazing on the (**berry** **bury**) trees that grew in the vicinity. It was only last (**week** **weak**) one had been seen running across the dusty (**road** **rode**) (**which** **witch**) runs along the side of the forest.

3. Complete each sentence using a homophone of the underlined word.

a. The <u>guest</u> won the prize as she _____ the correct answer.

b. On the packet of self-raising <u>flour</u> there is a picture of a red_____ .

c. My <u>hair</u> stood on end when the_____ ran between my legs.

d. The <u>poor</u> man began to_____ the cold tea into the cup.

e. I watched her <u>peer</u> at the ship as she stood on the_____ .

© P. Clutterbuck, Good Grammar! Book 3. This page may be reproduced for classroom use.

Homographs

A homograph is a word that is spelled the same as another word but has a different meaning.

1. Choose four words and write two sentences for each one. Make sure that each gives the word a different meaning.

> seal   palm   plane   prune   pupil   store   fine   safe

a. _____

_____

b. _____

_____

c. _____

_____

d. _____

_____

2. Unjumble the letters to make a word that has both meanings in the brackets.

a. tje   (plane/spurt of water)   _____

b. rbka   (tree covering/noise of a dog)   _____

c. lcaf   (young cow/lower leg)   _____

d. ewll   (not ill/water hole)   _____

e. rgvae   (serious/tomb)   _____

f. xbo   (container/spar)   _____

g. aball   (plaything/dance)   _____

h. iknd   (caring/type of thing)   _____

3. Think of a homograph that can fill both spaces in each sentence.

a. I am sure the money will be _____ now it is locked in the_____.

b. The police will_____you for speeding whether the weather is rainy or_____.

c. Mike_____ angrily when Ben broke the_____of his bike wheel.

© P. Clutterbuck, Good Grammar! Book 3. This page may be reproduced for classroom use.

Twin Words

Twin words are words that are often paired together, especially in speech. For example: *salt and pepper.*

1. Add a twin word from the box.

(less   sound   there   heels   thin   square   never   down)

a. head over _____   e. safe and _____
b. up and _____   f. here and _____
c. thick and _____   g. more or _____
d. now or _____   h. fair and _____

2. Complete each sentence using a twin word from the box.

(take   span   round   tongs   again   neck   furious   low)

a. The two dogs fought hammer and _____ over the bone.
b. The girls ran round and _____ the yard until they were tired.
c. The room looked spick and _____ after I cleaned it.
d. There has to be some give and _____ if we are to be fair.
e. We looked high and _____ but we couldn't find it.
f. The horses raced neck and _____ along the course.
g. The match was played at a fast and _____ pace.
h. I have told you again and _____ not to do it.

3. Complete the twin words.
a. fish and _____
b. bread and _____
c. salt and _____
d. hot and _____
e. knife and _____
f. safe and _____

© P. Clutterbuck, Good Grammar! Book 3. This page may be reproduced for classroom use.

Double Negatives

Name _____   **Grammar BLM** 86

If you want a sentence to have a negative meaning, do not put two negatives in it.
Do not say: I <u>didn't</u> see nothing.
Say: I <u>didn't see</u> anything.
**   I saw <u>nothing</u>.**

1. Circle the two negative words in these confusing sentences. Then write the sentence correctly to give a negative meaning.

a. I don't want nothing.

     _____

b. I can't find nothing.

     _____

c. He isn't going nowhere.

     _____

d. The new boy doesn't like nobody.

     _____

e. I don't want no vegetables.

     _____

f. The new teacher doesn't know nothing.

     _____

g. The children weren't allowed to play no games.

     _____

h. I have never read none of those books.

     _____

i. We have not been nowhere near the oval.

     _____

j. There wasn't none left for me.

     _____

© P. Clutterbuck, Good Grammar! Book 3. This page may be reproduced for classroom use.

Funny Signs

Briefly explain what is strange about each of these signs.

a. On a cake shop window

Homemade cakes—straight from the factory to you.

_____

_____

b. On a bakery window

Try our homemade pies—you'll never get better.

_____

_____

c. Outside a restaurant

Wanted—young person to wash dishes and two waiters.

_____

_____

d. Outside a hairdressing salon

Haircuts while you wait.

_____

_____

e. At a hardware store

Don't let lawn mowing kill you—let us do it for you.

_____

_____

f. Inside a supermarket

Instant soft drink in only 10 minutes.

_____

_____

© P. Clutterbuck, Good Grammar! Book 3. This page may be reproduced for classroom use.